I Can Do It!

A Micropedia of Living on Your Own

by Marian B. Latzko

Third edition

ISBN: 0-9651826-0-6

Library of Congress Catalog Card Number: 96-94294

Published by
Microlife
1610 W. Briarcliff Drive
Appleton, WI 54915-2837

Printed by
Palmer Publications, Inc.
PO Box 296
Amherst, WI 54406

Dedication

To my husband who has given me life's greatest gifts of love and encouragement
to complete my education when it was not "the thing to do."

To my children who have filled my life with meaning and pride
as they continue to share themselves with others.

To my grandchildren as they continue to learn.
(I expect greatness!)

To my fellow teachers and professionals
who have worked with me and continue to teach me.

To my students who were wonderful teachers themselves!

To God who has blessed my life.

To you, my readers!

Acknowledgment

Through my full life of learning, I could not begin to acknowledge all the writings, experiences, lectures, and relationships that have contributed to this book. I can only say thank you for the teaching and sharing of family, friends, teachers, students and community.

Special thanks go to:

- My illustrator, daughter Sally Kneeland, who interrupted her busy schedule of teaching and updating her career in computer and graphics to draw for this book. Her background in Family and Consumer Sciences and her own family give her background and understanding.

- My advertising helper, daughter Leslie Dent, who seems to find the right words to say so others can understand my purpose. Her background in newspaper editing and writing gives her talents to use.

- My husband, Bob, who is assisting in the next stage of this book, the "sell" and "distribute" part. His profession in engineering management gives him background to help.

- All other family members and friends who are supporting, encouraging and offering assistance as this project continues.

Table of Contents

You Can Do It!

Why I Wrote This Book

I believe in young people. I believe that they can do it on their own. I also believe that they can do it better if they have more information!

This book is my "trial balloon" for an alternative way to get needed information to young graduates who are testing their wings by living on their own.

Our schools have not found a way to teach students the practical information they need in their "real lives," and I've not found a way to get the information to them through the school systems. (I've even tried the political arena!) This book is my first alternative education attempt. Young people will tend to learn quickly and eagerly if they have the information at their fingertips when they really need it.

Families used to teach many of life's skills in their homes. Today's families are changing and often have little time or, sometimes, knowledge to teach the "how-to-do" of everyday living. Choices and decisions are increasingly complex. In the thinking process of decision making, the gathering and evaluating of information is important. This book was created to put under one cover much of the information that is helpful as young adults leave the nest. From this information their choices can be wiser.

I've recognized the importance of this missing knowledge through the years from my own family who have asked many times, "Mom, why don't you write a book?" I've also found the same need through working with potential dropouts, school-age mothers, and many types of students from elementary and high schools. Wherever I work with people in community activities or while creating programs, I recognize the growing importance of getting more information to individuals and families that will help them in their complex lives. This book offers a guide to help people create and follow a road map to reach their lives' goals and create a better quality of life.

I'm ever hopeful that our society will recognize the importance of applying the physical and social sciences through thinking skills for "real life" situations. The words family and thinking are now being heard repeatedly through the media and in our daily conversations. My profession of consumer and family sciences can help with the job.

So this book was created as a guide for families that are and families that will be.

I know they can do it!

How to Use This Book

This "micropedia of living on your own" is filled with information you will need when you're making decisions for yourself. Just check the index or chapter titles for what you want to know. It can be used as a planning tool, an educational process, and a resource for specific information.

Planning Tool!

Use the book to think and to plan. It will help you reach your goals and avoid some common mistakes.

• Use the book after you've been on your own for a short time or a long time. It will help you evaluate what you've done and give you more information with which to make decisions.

• Use the book before leaving home to live on your own. Planning what you will need, where you will live, how to find a compatible roommate or how to set up a credit rating are just a few things that can help you. Preplanning your finances can point to success, delay, or failure as you follow your dreams.

Special challenge to young adults: Ask your parents and friends to read it, too, and then discuss it together before you leave home.

Educational Process!

This book can be used for education in high schools, technical schools, colleges, alternative schools and home schools. It can be used just for the joy of knowledge and the pleasure of reading it cover to cover.

Your only REAL security comes from the knowledge you have in your head!

Resource!

The book can become dog-eared by looking up such questions as "how-to":
  • take stain out of a carpet
  • avoid pink laundry
  • avoid burglars
  • start a diet
  • plan a trip to Europe
  • balance your checkbook
  • wash a sweater
  • save money
  • sub-let an apartment
  • choose a mattress
  • defrost a refrigerator
  • find a doctor.

(There are tear-out sheets at the end of the book that you can reproduce for your use.)

Budgeting To Make Money Stretch

"How can I budget my money so there's enough to go around?"

The first thing to do is to decide what you really want to accomplish in your life. When you plan, you can put your money to work. Your decisions can help you accomplish your dreams. The decisions can be made by default… letting others make decisions for you by just taking things as they come… or you can make decisions by planning actions of your own.

"People don't plan to fail. They fail to plan!"

A good spending plan can help you avoid money problems that could keep you from reaching your goals. The plan you make can't immediately cure money problems that started some time ago, but it can help with better planning.

There's a long life ahead, not just a year or two. The decisions you make today will affect your future.

So…first make a road map for your life with goals along the way. Then you can make a budget to help you get there. **The time to start is now!**

"You will never get where you want to go if you don't know where you're going!"

#1 Set Goals!

As you make your plans, consider your goals. There will be goals that you need for the *short term* (1-4 weeks), *medium term* (2-12 months), and *long term* (more than a year). After writing these down, apply them to the amount of money you have. Keep your goals visible. Look at them often, especially if you start to stray from your budget. You can reset plans, but the change should be worth it.

SHORT TERM FINANCIAL GOAL
(1-4 weeks)

MY GOAL: _____

ESTIMATED COST: _____ MONEY STILL NEEDED: _____ TARGET DATE: _____ WEEKLY AMOUNT: _____

STEPS TO TAKE TO GET TO MY GOAL: _____

_____

_____

_____

WHERE TO GET HELP TO ACCOMPLISH MY GOAL: _____

_____

_____

_____

MEDIUM TERM FINANCIAL GOAL
(2-12 months)

MY GOAL:_____

ESTIMATED COST: _____ MONEY STILL NEEDED: _____ TARGET DATE: _____ WEEKLY AMOUNT: _____

MONTHLY ACTIVITIES TO HELP SAVE TOWARD GOAL: _____

_____

_____

_____

OTHER WAYS OF ACHIEVING MY GOAL: _____

_____

_____

_____

LONG TERM FINANCIAL GOAL
(More than one year)

MY GOAL: _____

ESTIMATED COST: _____ MONEY STILL NEEDED: _____ TARGET DATE: _____ WEEKLY AMOUNT: _____

STEPS TO TAKE TO GET TO MY GOAL: _____
_____
_____
_____

PERSONS WHO CAN HELP ME REACH MY GOAL: _____
_____
_____
_____

FURTHER INFORMATION THAT I NEED TO ACCOMPLISH MY GOAL: _____
_____
_____
_____

OTHER WAYS I CAN ACCOMPLISH MY GOAL: _____   COST OF EACH:
_____
_____
_____

TIMETABLE TO ACCOMPLISH MY GOAL: _____
_____
_____
_____
_____

#2 Check Your Income

List all of your income resources so you know how much you have to spend. Include any money that you have available.

TOTAL INCOME STATEMENT

SOURCE	PER MONTH	PER YEAR	AVAILABLE ONLY ONCE
TAKE-HOME PAY PART-TIME JOB			
TAKE-HOME PAY FULL-TIME JOB			
SAVINGS			
ALLOWANCES			
GIFTS			
INTEREST			
STOCKS/BONDS			
TAX REFUNDS			
SCHOLARSHIPS			
GOVERNMENT SUBSIDIES			
LOANS			
OTHER			
TOTALS			

#3 Figure Your Expenses

There are different kinds of expenses to be considered when budgeting. *Fixed expenses* are expenses that must be paid regularly such as rent, credit card payments, insurance, utilities, taxes, social security, and loans. (Make *savings* a fixed expense or you may never save to meet your goals. It's part of the plan!) *Flexible expenses* are expenses that vary in amount each month such as food, clothing, recreation, and gasoline. Things like utilities can change too. Figure your fixed expenses and subtract them from the total amount of money you have as income. When you find out what you have left for flexible expenses, you can set limits. Try it!

FIGURING YOUR FIXED EXPENSES

RENT	$_____
TAXES	_____
SOCIAL SECURITY (FICA)	_____
LOAN PAYMENTS	_____
CREDIT CARD PAYMENTS	_____
INSURANCE	_____
SAVINGS	_____
TUITION	_____
OTHER	_____
TOTAL FIXED EXPENSES	$_____
TOTAL INCOME	$_____
MINUS TOTAL FIXED EXPENSE	– $_____
AMOUNT LEFT FOR FLEXIBLE EXPENSES	= $_____

FIGURING YOUR FLEXIBLE EXPENSES

FOOD	$_____
EATING OUT	_____
TRANSPORTATION	_____
BOOKS/MAGAZINES	_____
RECREATION	_____
DONATIONS	_____
CLOTHING	_____
LAUNDRY/CLEANING	_____
DUES	_____
PERSONAL CARE	_____
MEDICAL/DENTAL	_____
VACATIONS	_____
FURNISHINGS	_____
GIFTS	_____
CLOTHING	_____
OTHER	_____
TOTAL FLEXIBLE EXPENSES	$_____

FIGURING IF YOU'VE BALANCED INCOME AND EXPENSES

TOTAL FIXED EXPENSES	$_____
PLUS TOTAL FLEXIBLE EXPENSES	+ _____
TOTAL EXPENSES	$_____
TOTAL INCOME	$_____
MINUS TOTAL EXPENSES	– _____
DIFFERENCE	$_____

If you have extra money left, it is easy to find ways to use it. If there is a loss, it's time to choose. Do I eat or do I play? Do I pay the utility bill or live without heat? Must I borrow? Do I stop credit card payments and pay late fees? Be realistic. Consider finding new resources and cutting expenses:

- Get a second job.
- Take time off from school and save for awhile.
- Stay with family for awhile and save.
- "Housesit" for someone.
- Borrow (Dangerous!)
- Sell something.
- Barter for what you need.

#4 Figure Ways to Cut Your Expenses

When you've created your first budget and find that there is not enough money to go around, figure ways to cut expenses so you won't end up in debt.

USE THE ECONOMIC PRINCIPLE OF OPPORTUNITY COST

Ask yourself when tempted to buy: "If I buy this what else will I not have the opportunity to buy?" This gives you some comparisons. You may prefer one thing rather than another.

SUGGESTIONS FOR CUTTING FLEXIBLE EXPENSES

Food
- Carefully look at food budget. Stop "eating out" and buying "junk foods".
- Don't shop when you're hungry. Avoid impulse shopping.
- Consider carrying your lunch.

Shopping
- Avoid or delay new purchases.
- Don't carry money with you, and avoid being tempted to buy.
- Buy less expensive brands when purchasing.
- Stay out of stores unless you need to be there to buy.
- Buy only on sale. Shop for best prices.
- Cut up credit cards and shop only with cash.

Budget
- Watch daily expenses closely, but don't be discouraged by keeping track of every penny.
- Allow yourself only a certain allowance for spending—Follow it!

Recreation
- Plan "no cost" or "low cost" activities (join community groups, volunteers, teams).
- Review newspapers for ideas.
- Share or borrow equipment (consider buying used equipment).
- Turn recreation into a money maker (i.e. ski patrol, usher at theatre performances).

Transportation
- Find a different car that uses less gasoline and oil and needs fewer repairs.
- Repair your car yourself.
- Carpool, walk, bike, or use public transportation.

SUGGESTIONS FOR CUTTING FIXED EXPENSES

Rent
- Find less expensive place to rent.
- Find another roommate.
- Ask landlord if you can do repairs or maintenance in exchange for rent.

Insurance
- Examine insurance to see if you're overinsured. Find less expensive insurance.
- Check to see if the place you work has a way to insure you.

Transportation
- Trade your present car for one that is more economical.
- Sell your car.

Rearrange Credit Payments
- Contact creditors to make new arrangements for smaller payments.
- Borrow to pay important bills that are due. (Dangerous!)
- Consolidate your bills.

Get Help
- Talk to a credit counselor. Find free services through the Yellow Pages and/or talk with social service agencies, legal aid societies, public and private family service agencies, Consumer Credit Counseling Services. Find who sponsors programs, charges, and how plan operates. Check with Better Business Bureau.
- See if your family is willing to help.

> **Review all chapters of this book to find detailed ways to save money. Each chapter gives information to help make decisions that save dollars and resources.**

#5 Create a Budget

Keep track of the way you actually spend money. A quick efficient way is to fold a paper into eight sections. Label each section for a day of the week. Carry it in your billfold and keep track of everything you spend each day. At the end of the week, total expenses. This spending pattern record will help you to see where the money goes and to take the next step of budget planning.

When you know your fixed expenses and your flexible expenses, you can make some adjustments and do a real budget plan. Things will not always go as planned, so watch what you planned to spend each month and what you actually spent. Then you can plan more efficiently the next month. **If you review your total budget closely at the end of three months, adjustments can be made to help avoid crises that can keep you from reaching your goals.** (There are budget sheets at the end of the book that you can use to create a full year's plan.)

THREE MONTH FINANCIAL PLAN						
FIXED EXPENSES:	Month 1 Planned	Actual	Month 2 Planned	Actual	Month 3 Planned	Actual
Social Security						
Rent						
Taxes						
Loans						
Credit card payments						
Savings						
Emergency fund*						
Reserve fund*						
Utilities: Gas/Electricity						
Telephone						
Pledges						
Renter's insurance						
Auto insurance						
Life insurance						
Medical insurance						
Water						
Other						
FLEXIBLE EXPENSES:	Month 1 Planned	Actual	Month 2 Planned	Actual	Month 3 Planned	Actual
Food						
Eating out						
Clothing						
Transportation, bus						
Automobile expenses						
Recreation						

	Month 1 Planned	Actual	Month 2 Planned	Actual	Month 3 Planned	Actual
Laundry/cleaning						
Newspapers/books						
Tuitions/education						
Books/supplies						
Dues						
Furnishings						
Cleaning supplies						
Personal care						
Hobbies						
Gifts						
Vacations						
Medical expenses						
Other						
Total for months						

* Especially as you are beginning, it is important to start building an emergency fund for unexpected expenses and a reserve fund for expenses that are paid in lumps rather than monthly.

SUMMARY...to evaluate your three-month spending pattern, subtract to see what's left over.

Total actual monthly income average
(Add three-month totals and divide by 3) $_____
MINUS total actual monthly fixed expense average
(Add three-month totals and divide by 3)   −_____
Total amount left for flexible expenses
after three-month period $_____

NOW COMPARE:

Actual amount spent for flexible expenses
(Add three-month totals and divide by 3) $_____
MINUS actual monthly amount left
for flexible expenses after three-month period   −_____

Total left over* $_____

*If this number is negative, you have work to do. Reset your priorities or goals and readjust your spending patterns.

If this number is positive, add the amount to your savings, emergency fund, or investments.

#6 Evaluate the Budget

Continue to evaluate your budget as you go along and change it as necessary. Also evaluate whether you are reaching your goals by checking your previous planning regularly. When checking your original goals, think through your values and your priorities. Sometimes changes will be necessary. Review the whole process if you are not satisfied with your progress. You may even want to ask for help.

If You Keep Track of Your Budget for a Year

If you keep track of your spending for a full year using the sheets at the end of the book, you can use the following summary to evaluate and see how well you did. This will help you with your next year's planning.

SUMMARY

Expenses/Income	Planned	Actual
Total income		
Monthly average fixed expenses		
Subtract to get amount available for flexible expenses		

YEARLY FINANCIAL PLAN BUDGET SUMMARY

FIXED EXPENSES	Planned	Actual
Social Security (FICA)		
Rent		
Taxes		
Loan payments		
Credit card payments		
Savings		
Emergency fund*		
Reserve fund*		
Utilities		
Telephone		
Pledges		
Renter's insurance		
Auto insurance		
Life insurance		
Medical insurance		
Water		
Other		
Total fixed expenses		
FLEXIBLE EXPENSES		
Food		
Eating out		
Clothing		
Transportation, bus or taxi		
Automobile expenses		
Recreation		
Laundry/cleaning		
Newspapers/books		
Tuitions/education		
Books/supplies		
Dues		
Furnishings		
Cleaning supplies		
Personal care		
Hobbies		
Gifts		
Vacations		
Medical expenses		
Total flexible expenese		
TOTAL YEARLY EXPENSES		

YEARLY BUDGET SUMMARY

Total Income	$_____
Minus the Total Fixed & Flexible Expenses	– _____
Balance	$_____ *

* If this balance is negative, you have work to do to reset your priorities or goals. If it is positive, you can add to your savings, emergency fund or investments.

Budgeting Hints

• **Envelope budgeting** may work for you. Place money for bills to be paid in envelopes marked "Newspaper," "Laundry/Dry-cleaning," "Hair Cuts," etc. If you are concerned with cash in the house, prewrite checks and put them in the envelopes.

• **Understanding Life Cycle Financial Tasks** helps you view the use of money through your whole life.

LIFE CYCLE FINANCIAL TASKS LIST

Ages 18-24	Ages 25-34
Establish household	Child bearing, rearing
Career training	Expanded housing needs
Financial independence	Additional protection coverage
Establish financial identity	Provide for expanding career/education
Purchase risk coverage	Invest wisely to cover future costs
Establish savings	
Develop effective financial record keeping	

Ages 34-44	Ages 45-54
Build educational fund	Provide for higher education of children
Plan for retirement	

Ages 55-64	Ages 65+
Meet expanding needs of parents &/or dependents	Finalize plans for sharing estate
Consolidate assets and plan for retirement	

Using Banks and Credit

"How can I keep my money safe and have it work for me?"

BANKS

Banks can be used to help you manage your money and to help it grow. Banks help keep your records, give you opportunities to save, keep your money safe, give special services, make loans, and advise about growth investments. If you want your money to work for you to help meet your goals, comparison shop for services, understand how banks and credit work, and plan carefully.

Types of Banks

Banks are controlled by the government to protect your money. The Federal Deposit Insurance Corporation (FDIC) insures deposits up to $100,000 in banks. There is also a similar service provided to savings and loan associations and credit unions. Make sure your bank is protected. Banks are often chosen for convenience of location or services. Shop around. Services and costs differ.

Commercial or full service banks provide individuals and businesses with a full range of services: loans, money deposits, trust services, savings, credit cards, traveler's checks, safety deposit boxes.

Mutual savings banks are non-profit and are owned by depositors. They offer varied services including checking and some commercial loans (i.e. home improvement, home and commercial mortgages).

Savings and loan or building and loan banks may be owned by depositors or by stockholders. They have various services, but the main service is loans on homes for mortgages and improvements. They are insured by FSLIC (Federal Savings and Loan Insurance Corporation).

Private banks are rare. They are usually partnerships. They take deposits, are not insured, and do not generally make small loans. They may pay higher interest rates, but are more risky.

Credit unions are set up by special interest groups and are owned by their members (i.e. trade unions).

Members set rules by voting. Deposits are insured by various groups. Services vary: regular banking services, discounts, group insurance, special information.

Checking Accounts

Advantages of having checking accounts include: valid receipts, spending record, awareness of amount of money left, convenience of not carrying money, and paying bills by mail. Compare bank services by figuring and comparing the costs. Look at:

- Availability and cost of services.
- Process and cost of "bouncing" or cancelling a check.
- Return of cancelled checks (Is a charge made for copies except for IRS purposes?)
- Direct deposit service and time frame for crediting account.
- Cost of checks (Banks may have free checks unless fancy ones are ordered).
- Interest given on savings and checking accounts.
- If checks can be started with large number to avoid check cashing difficulty of a new account.
- Time lapse required before new account can be used.

Regular checking accounts require you to pay a small amount for each check you write. This may be the least expensive way for you to do your banking if you write very few checks per month.

Special checking accounts may require you to keep a minimum balance in the account. These usually allow free check writing. Sometimes the requirement is a minimum balance in a savings account for the free checking. If you drop below the minimum balance required, a service charge is made for checks.

NOW accounts (negotiable order of withdrawal) tie checking and savings together with no money kept in the checking account. Funds are automatically transferred from the savings account when checks are written. You will receive a set percentage of interest from the savings account. Charges are made if a high enough balance isn't maintained. Interest can be figured on average daily balance, minimum balance, or other method.

Super NOW accounts pay a rate of interest usually comparable to certificates of deposit (CD). They require funds to be tied up for varying time periods. Usually a large minimum balance is required to earn the higher interest rate. If the balance falls below the requirement, the interest is dropped.

Free checking accounts are not easy to find, but are available in some communities. There is no required minimum balance or service charge except for "bounced" checks.

Transaction accounts require no minimum balance. All funds earn interest. All transactions have charges (i.e. checks, deposits, withdrawals, transfers). A report is sent each month. If the transactions are greater than interest earned, a charge is made on the difference. If transactions are smaller than interest earned, the difference is added to your account.

Share draft accounts are available with savings accounts through credit unions. A draft is used that is similar to a check.

HOW TO WRITE CHECKS

1. Write in black or blue ink. (Avoid erasable ink pens!)
2. Write clearly. (If numbers are not clear, the written amount of the check will be used.)
3. Always start writing at far left of line so changes can't be made by someone else.
4. Always sign your name as written on bank records. NEVER sign your name if there are empty spaces on the check.

5. Indicate the purpose for the check to help your records (i.e. account numbers, time periods for rent payments, insurance policy numbers).
6. If you make a mistake, mark "VOID" across the check and rip it up before throwing it away.

HOW TO RECORD CHECKS ON CHECK REGISTER

1. <u>Immediately record</u> all written checks, deposits and ATM transactions in check register. Then figure the balance so you don't overspend.
2. Record date, check number, and purpose of checks.
3. Record date and source of deposits. If using ATM machine, record deposit or withdrawal and location of machine used. Keep deposit and withdrawal slips.

HOW TO RECONCILE YOUR CHECKBOOK WITH YOUR BANK STATEMENT

Reconcile your account balance with the bank statement each month to make sure there are no errors.

Avoid spending money you don't have and writing "bouncing checks" that cost money and harm credit ratings. Check the amount of money you have left in your checkbook account every month with the bank statement that is sent to you. Bank statements vary in form. Each, however, includes a record of your cashed (cancelled) checks and other debits and deposits with check numbers, dates, and amounts. Here is an example.

STATEMENT

John Jones
250 Cozy Cove Rd
Lodi MI 22566

Account Number   12679-08

Date of Statement   January 21,19__

PREVIOUS BALANCE	CHECKS AND CHARGES	NO. OF DEPOSITS	NO. OF CHECKS	DEPOSITS AND CREDITS	BALANCE AT THIS DATE
162.50	41.95	1	2	35.87	156.42

CHECK #	CHECKS AND OTHER CHARGES	DEPOSITS AND OTHER CREDITS	DATE	BALANCE
				162.50
		35.87	1/4	198.37
1023	12.95		1/6	185.42
1024	27.00		1/9	158.42
	2.00 (check charges)		1/19	156.42

1. In your check register, check box marked "T" for each cashed (cancelled) check that has been enclosed with your bank statement. Make sure any check amount, check register, and bank statement agree.
2. Look on the bank statement for any bank charges. Write these charges in your checkbook register and subtract them from the balance. (If you have a NOW account, look on the statement for any interest on the bank statement. Add this amount to your register for a new balance.)
3. On the back of your bank statement there will be a method of checking your check register with the bank statement balance. It will direct you to:

   a) Enter statement balance as shown on bank statement. $156.42
   b) Add deposits made after the bank statement was issued.   + 74.78
       231.20
   c) Subtract total of all outstanding checks (checks that you wrote that are not recorded on the bank statement plus any checks from a previous month that were not cashed)   - 16.54
       $ 214.66*

*The bank statement and your register should have the same balance. If not, recheck figures. (If you find an error that you can't correct, call the bank.)

HOW TO ENDORSE CHECKS

A **special endorsement** allows you to sign a check you received over to someone else.

A **restrictive endorsement** means that the check can be used only as directed. (i.e. *For deposit only* means it can only be deposited in your account. If you mail a check, it is best to use this endorsement in case the check is lost.)

A **blank endorsement** is your signature only. Once it is signed it is the same as money since anyone can cash it.

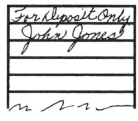

SPECIAL ENDORSEMENT

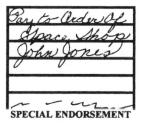

RESTRICTIVE ENDORSEMENT

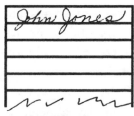

BLANK ENDORSEMENT

Savings Instruments

Savings are an important part of your financial plan. Follow the PYF Plan, "Pay Yourself First," before you pay other bills. If you do not create this safety net, you may not be able to carry out your goals and protect yourself in case of unexpected problems. The amount you save depends on the goals and time line you have allowed yourself. You need funds for your goals and an emergency fund that can be used immediately when needed.

You can work toward saving enough to start out by staying home a while longer, sharing your living space, getting extra jobs, or investing wisely. It may seem that saving money doesn't help your assets to grow if you have only a little to invest. Here is a chart to give you some idea of how even small investments grow.

$5.00 PER WEEK PLAN
(invested at 5¹/4% interest compounded daily)

Weekly	After 1 yr.	After 3 yrs.	After 5 yrs.	After 10 yrs.	After 20 yrs.
$5	$ 267.16	$ 845.95	$1,489.54	$ 3,431.69	$ 9,265.67
10	534.32	1,691.89	2,979.08	6,863.37	18,531.35
15	801.48	2,537.84	4,468.62	10,295.06	27,797.02
25	1,335.79	4,229.74	7,447.71	17,158.43	46,328.37

If you want a simple way to estimate the way your money can grow, use the "Rule of 72":

- Divide 72 by the interest rate you expect to earn to see how many years it will take to double your money.
- Divide 72 by the number of years in which you want to double your money to get an estimate of the percentage you will need to earn to do this.

SAVINGS ACCOUNT TYPES

Passbook or statement savings accounts are available at most savings institutions. They offer low interest rates, immediate withdrawals, low minimum balance or no balance requirements.

Credit union accounts are available only at credit unions. There may be some restrictions on the account. Interest rates are usually low to medium.

Certificates of deposit commit funds for a specific period of time (30 days to 8 years). You may take the money out, but you pay a penalty if cashed before maturity. Longer term CD's usually have higher rates. Rates usually lock in, which may be an advantage or disadvantage.

Money market accounts have variable interest rates. There is a minimum deposit required. If the account drops below minimum, the interest usually goes to lower rates. Often transactions are limited in number. There may be checking privileges.

Money market funds are available from a mutual fund or stockbroker. They generally offer a high comparative yield, but rates fluctuate. Check writing is often limited. Funds are not insured. There is no penalty for withdrawal. No sales commission is required.

Christmas Club accounts are offered for year-end or holiday use. The bank usually sends a check to the depositor at year's end. The money can be deposited directly into another account.

Cookie Jar funds are a tried and true method of saving. Drop your change into a jar and watch it grow.

Before choosing a savings account, you should ask:
- Is a minimum balance required?
- Does the annual yield fluctuate or stay fixed?
- Is interest compounded; if so when and on what balance? How often?
- Is it possible to withdraw funds or transfer funds to another account?
- What is the cost of transferring funds?
- Are there any extra fees?
- Is account covered by FDIC insurance?

INVESTMENT OPPORTUNITIES

Banks offer investment counseling if you have enough money to invest for profit. Comparison shop.
- **U.S. Savings bonds:** U.S. government investment with set maturity date at price below face value.
- **Certificate of deposit (CD):** Specific amount of money for set time and interest rate.
- **Treasury issues:** Treasury department bills, notes, or bonds of $1,000 to $1 million that mature from 30 days to 5 years.
- **Bonds:** Corporation or government certificates of debt that pay interest plus original investment on a specified date.

- **Stocks:** Share of ownership of a company. Value increases or decreases according to success of the corporation.
- **Mutual funds:** Pooling of dollars that are placed in various investments by professionals.
- **Commodities:** Speculative contracts on future world demands of basics such as food and metals.

Credit

Credit has become an established way of doing business today. It can help you reach your goals or can keep you from reaching them. It becomes a part of your total financial plan. A good credit rating is necessary for emergencies when you must borrow money. Since credit is based on future earnings, it should be used with great care. You can't read the future.

Credit is tempting and dangerous...especially when you have little money to do all of the things that you want to do. **Credit seems simple but isn't.** You as a consumer are encouraged to purchase with promises such as "Only $12.00 per month!" without information about the total cost of an item that may end up costing more than the original price. Long-term credit can be more expensive than a direct bank loan. Buying more than you can afford can destroy your credit rating so you can't get credit when you need it. Credit ratings last for several years, so mistakes are not easy to erase. Buying on credit takes discipline that many people do not have.

When thinking of buying on credit consider the "opportunity cost" of the item. Ask yourself, "What will I not have the opportunity to buy, if I buy this?" "What would I rather have?" "Will this purchase help me reach my goals?" Other things to think about:

- Decide if you are impulse buying with an "it would be nice to have" attitude rather than real need.
- Consider other alternatives.
- Know the full cost of credit before accepting it.
- Consider the whole cost of the article by including the credit charges.
- Comparison shop for lowest interest costs and consider how to pay bill off as early as possible.

If you absolutely must use credit, a rule of thumb recommends that the total credit payments you have per month should not exceed 15% to 20% of your income after taxes and housing have been paid.

Establish credit so you have it when you need it. There will be times that you really benefit from borrowing, especially when buying large items such as a car or a house. You can establish credit by:

- Creating a steady work record on a job.
- Always paying your bills promptly.
- Never bouncing a check.
- Starting a savings account and a checking account.
- Applying for credit at institutions such as department stores, banks, or credit unions. (You may need a friend or relative to co-sign.)
- Buying something or taking out a loan, then repaying promptly or ahead of time.
- Getting your name on a prompt paying relative's account.
- Repaying a student loan ahead of time with a few extra payments.

If you are denied credit, find out why. If it's because of information supplied by a credit bureau, find the problem. A credit report can be requested within 30 days of receiving a denial letter. (In case of an error, credit bureaus must notify any creditor who has checked your file in the last month.) Talk with the companies involved. If you can't agree, you may file a statement of up to 100 words telling your side of the story.

Check your credit ratings with credit bureaus every 3-4 years for incompletes and inaccuracies. As you are starting your credit, you may want to check yearly. Look in the telephone directory for "Credit and Debt Counseling Services" or ask for a name to contact at a bank or place of business. The three main credit bureaus are:

EXPERIAN   (formerly TRW)
Telephone: 1-888-397-3742
1-800-682-7654
PO Box 2106   Allen, TX 75013

TRANS-UNION CONSUMER CREDIT
Telephone: 1-800-916-8800
PO Box 34012
1561 East Orangethrope
Fullerton, CA 92831

CSC CREDIT SERVICES, INC
Telephone: 1-800-759-5979
P.O. Box 674406
Houston, TX 77267

Credit ratings are created by credit bureaus who sell information to banks and retailers who grant credit. The bureau keeps track of the history of payment of all bills and records any bills that are overdue or any actions taken to collect bills. Some creditors use a scoring system to predict credit risk. The information includes age, income, debt, assets, and reliability of paying bills on time.

Negative information can be reported for only seven years, except for bankruptcies. These can be reported indefinitely if you want to take out a large loan or apply for a good paying job.

If you are in financial trouble:
- Don't wait to be turned over to a debt collector.
- Ask your creditors for a smaller payment plan.
- Talk to a credit counselor to see about consolidating your debts so there is only one payment in a smaller amount per month. (Check the cost of the loan and know that you can meet the payments.) Consumer credit counselors should be listed in the *Yellow Pages* under social service agencies, legal aid societies, or consumer credit organizations.
- Sell your car to pay off a car loan debt. (If car is repossessed, you may pay additional fees.)
- Find a part-time job to pay outstanding bills.
- Look at all alternatives for cutting your budget immediately.

CREDIT CARDS

Many people get in serious financial difficulty because of overuse of credit cards. Many end up ceremoniously cutting them up! The most important rule is **"Do not buy what you cannot afford!"**

If You Choose To Use A Credit Card, comparison shop. Consider:
- Fees required for credit card use.
- When bills are due and what the grace period is for the payment of the bill.
- APR (annual percentage rate) that is charged and method used for charges: average daily balance, previous balance, or adjusted balance.
- Requirements for purchase of insurances such as disability, accident, or death.
- The credit limit (amount you can borrow).
- Reputation of issuer of the card and the card's acceptance by various businesses.

If you buy with a credit card and pay your statement promptly with no interest fee, you receive free credit for a few days, depending on when you purchase compared to the billing date.

Keep your credit cards safe and avoid charges made by someone else.
- Watch your credit card after giving it to a clerk. Take it back promptly and check that it's yours.
- Tear up carbons, if there are any, when you get your credit card receipt.
- Never sign a blank receipt. Draw a line through any blank spaces above the total on receipt.
- When you receive a bill, check against your receipts and note any unauthorized charges or errors.
- If you question charges, notify the issuer of the card right away. Then, before 60 days have passed, write your concerns and send in separate envelope.
- Never give your credit card number to anyone over the phone unless you've made the call.

- Sign a new credit card immediately. Cut up old credit cards. Cut up and return any unwanted cards.
- When you've cleared all charge slips, rip them up in tiny pieces so your number can't be found.

If your credit card is lost or stolen, report it immediately by phone to the company or bank that issued it. (Keep the telephone number of the company and the card number in a place that is easily accessible, but not with the credit card!) Then write to the issuer of the card stating the number of the card and the date that it was lost. This should protect you from any charges that are made on the card by anyone else. There is usually no charge for the loss, but if there is, it should be no more than $50.00.

CREDIT ACCOUNTS

Regular or 30 day accounts must be paid in full each month on the date designated on the bill. No finance charges are paid if the bill is paid on time.

Revolving or optional accounts allow you to charge to a set dollar limit. You pay a specified amount plus interest on the remaining balance each month. You can pay the balance in full or in a smaller percentage balance.

Installment or time payment accounts are paid in predetermined amounts over a set period of time.

LOANS

Family loans are often an excellent source of funds. Trust is the most important part of this type of loan. The loans do, however, have emotions attached.

Education loans are available through the government. The STAFFORD loans do not require interest to be paid until the loans are due. The government pays the interest during this period of time. For information, contact college financial aid offices or call NELLIE MAE at 1-800-9-TUITION.

Bank loans usually require collateral such as a house or car (when you are buying one), stocks, or bonds.

Credit union loans are available to members only. The rates are usually the lowest you can find.

Small loan or finance company loans usually have high rates because they loan to poor credit risk people. Check the reputation of any finance company.

Pawn shops are quick to use but very expensive. They do not report to credit bureaus.

Protecting Your Money and Your Future

"What can I do to protect myself from unexpected financial problems?"

INSURANCE

Insurance helps you to plan for the unknown. Accidents, death, fire, theft, economic changes, and illness happen. If you have no protection, you can be in financial trouble for years. Policies available from the government, employer, or family are limited. It is best to create a personal insurance plan that will give you all of the protection that you need no matter what the future holds.

Where to Get Insurance

Family

When you start out on your own, your family's insurance does not normally cover you unless there are provisions in the policy. Check to see what coverage you will retain. Once you have reached the age of eighteen and are off on your own, **you** are responsible for your own well-being. When in school, medical or household insurance of your family may cover you for some time. There are limitations to consider if you marry, become pregnant, or drop out of school.

Employment

If you are covered with life and medical insurance through your employment, consider what will happen when you leave. If you become uninsurable due to illness, you may not be able to get insurance again. There may be alternatives of continuing the insurance when your employment stops, probably at higher rates. Check these limits and see if you need to carry additional insurance. Consider the worst scenario.

Yourself

If you are not covered with insurance by family or employment, choose a recommended insurance agent in the same way you would choose a doctor. If you already have family coverage, an agent can help you look at alternatives and also help you understand.

Types of Insurance

AUTOMOBILE INSURANCE

Automobile insurance is required in most states. Shop for this insurance the same as you would any other important purchase that you make.

Liability insurance provides protection when you are at fault (liable) in an accident. The coverage in a policy is designated by three numbers (i.e. 10/20/5).

- The first number tells the amount of money paid for bodily injury for one person (i.e.$10,000).
- The second number is the amount paid for liability for all injuries in one accident (i.e. $20,000).
- The third number is the amount of property damage that is covered (i.e. $5,000).

Collision insurance pays for damage to the automobile even if you are responsible. There is usually a deductible clause included that requires you to pay a certain amount of the cost of any accident (i.e. $100, $200, $500). A lower deductible amount is more costly since the insurance company must pay more of the costs.

Comprehensive or Physical Damage pays for the costs of damage to your car not covered by collision insurance (i.e. theft, hail, vandalism).

Medical Payment pays for such things as hospital expenses, funerals, X-rays, and medicines for persons in your car. It usually covers you if you are driving someone else's car, walking, or riding a bicycle.

Uninsured motorist covers you as a driver or a hit-and-run victim if you have an accident with someone who doesn't have insurance.

No-Fault insurance is available in certain states. It protects you no matter who is at fault. Rates are generally lower on this insurance.

Government insurance is available, usually through a state, for those who are not insurable under usual policies, and/or have poor driving records. This is very expensive insurance because of the risk.

MOTORCYCLE INSURANCE

Motorcycle insurance is very much like automobile insurance. Since there are several important differences and limits in different policies, check carefully with your insurance agent.

HEALTH INSURANCE

Changes are occurring rapidly in the health insurance business. It is best to check with various agents to see what is best for you when you are ready for the insurance. Then you should keep aware of changes affecting health insurance.

Health insurance is usually available through your employer in some form. Check benefits carefully to see that coverage meets all of your needs and that the policy can continue when you leave your job. (An unexpected illness could make you uninsurable with another company.) You may be covered by your family's health policy if you are still in school. Student health plans are offered at most universities and colleges. Check into these to see if they will meet your needs. There are various types of insurance.

HMO (Health Maintenance Organization) provides a wide range of medical services from routine check ups to surgery for a fixed fee. Cost is generally lower than standard group insurance. You must use the doctors provided by the organization or pay for an outside doctor on your own.

PMO (Preferred Provider Organizations) medical plan is similar to an HMO, but allows patients to choose from a list of "preferred" physicians or to pay a "non-preferred doctor" on fee-for-service basis.

Hospital insurance pays for such things as room and board, nursing service, hospital services, lab tests, oxygen and drugs, and medicines.

Surgical insurance pays for doctor's fees for surgery done in or out of the hospital.

Regular medical insurance pays all or part of doctor's fees except for surgery.

Major medical insurance pays for the cost of extended illness not covered by normal insurance.

Disability insurance pays a designated amount of income to cover the loss of wages if you become unable to work.

LIFE INSURANCE

Life insurance is used for paying bills incurred before death or as a protection of dependents. It can also be used for forced savings and equity for loans. There are three basic types of life insurance. Each type pays a set amount of money to the beneficiaries at the time of death.

Term insurance is the least expensive type and is most popular with young adults. Protection is for a limited time such as a year and is then renewable at the set amount of payment. This payment may rise with age. If the policy is not renewed or if payments are not paid on time, the policy is dropped. This insurance does not have value at the end of the term designated. Sometimes this type of policy is used to insure a mortgage or other costly contract if the owner dies. Some term policies are *convertible* which allows you to trade the term policy for a whole life or endowment policy before the end of the conversion period. The new policy will cost more.

Level term insurance has premium (cost) increases each time policy is renewed (usually 1 to 5 years). Check if policy is "guaranteed renewable" so it can be in force if a health problem arises.

Decreasing term insurance gives less insurance as years pass. This is often used for mortgage insurance (when mortgage is smaller, less insurance is needed).

Whole life insurance includes a savings plan with insurance protection. As long as policy terms are followed, protection continues for life. Some policies have cash value that can either be borrowed or cashed in. Some policies continue for a set period of time such as 20 years or to age 65. At the end of the time the policy is "paid up" so that no more payments are necessary. This type of policy can be used as collateral on a loan.

Limited payment insurance has premiums paid for a set number of years or to a certain age, such as 65. The insurance stays in force for life.

Endowment insurance gives a sum of money or income to the holder of the policy at a set time. If the policy holder dies, the money goes to a beneficiary.

RENTER'S AND HOME OWNER'S INSURANCE

Renter's insurance covers personal possessions in a rented apartment or home. It may cover living expenses if home is not habitable. Items such as expensive jewelry, cameras and computers may need extra coverage. "Replacement coverage" covers replacement of items, not just a portion of used items. A landlord should have some coverage for disasters, but a tenant is responsible if a fire is caused by his/her negligence. Tenants are responsible for their own belongings.

Homeowner's insurance covers not only personal possessions, but also the home. All policies cover some personal liability for accidents that occur at the home to family members or guests. There are different forms of this type of policy. A *basic policy* covers only eight common perils such as fire, theft, aircraft, windstorm. A *broad policy* covers 18 risks and includes such things as collapse of a building, water damage, and freezing. A *comprehensive policy* includes all 18 risks plus specific exclusions from the other types of policies such as earthquake, war, nuclear accidents, or sewer backups.

Some General Things to Consider with Insurance

- Read policies each year to see that they are keeping up with the cost of inflation and your needs.
- Do not lie on insurance applications. Usually preexisting conditions are not covered; however, some policies begin coverage if no treatment is given for one or two years.
- Never sign an application for any policy until you have fully read and understood every part of the policy and its benefits. There should never be any blank spaces or incomplete answers recorded.
- Any policy should be delivered to you within 30 days. If it is not, contact the insurer. If you don't hear within 60 days, contact the state department of insurance.
- If you consider switching policies, be aware of new waiting periods and new exclusions.

- Remember that "dread disease" policies such as cancer insurance are not the same as regular insurance.
- Save mailing costs and money on policy premiums by paying annually or quarterly.
- Photograph or video your belongings noting the costs so you have records for filing a claim.
- When taking out a new policy, take advantage of the "free look" offer. Look policy over, then ask for a refund if you don't want it. If you do this, **be sure** to cancel the policy within the allowed time!
- Don't carry overlap insurance. Benefits are usually limited to a coordination of the policies to cover only 100% of the cost.

Filing Insurance Claims

If you need to file a claim, first ask your insurance agent or broker what the process is.

- If the claim is for an auto accident, be sure to get the names, addresses, and phone numbers of all persons in the car, especially the driver. Make a diagram of the accident. **Don't say that you are at fault!**
- File the claim as soon as possible.
- Be aware of the insurance coverage of your policy.
- **DO NOT accept the claim check if you are not satisfied. DO NOTsign a claims release form. DO NOT be taken advantage of because of the emotions involved!**

Saving Your Records

Keeping good records becomes increasingly important. In today's electronic world, there are so many records kept, there are many chances for errors.

Tax returns and documenting materials should be kept indefinitely.

- IRS can go back for six years for gross underpayment of 25% or more.
- IRS can question and do routine audits for three years.
- IRS can go back indefinitely for alleged fraud or non-filing.

Life insurance policies should be kept at home in a metal box to avoid fire damage. Keep policy numbers in a separate place. If necessary, insurance companies can replace the policies.

Original legal papers should be kept in a safety deposit box. Copies and lists of contents should be kept at home. Legal papers include: birth certificates, marriage certificates, military records, stocks and bonds, adoption papers, divorce papers, citizenship papers, contracts, and wills. Copies of wills should also be kept with the lawyer who prepared it. (Valid handwritten wills are available at office supply stores for anyone wanting to write his/her own.) There should also be a copy at home along with a note of where the original is kept. Most states "freeze" contents of safety deposit boxes when a person dies until contents are inventoried by an official and a family member.

Social security records should be kept and checked at least every three years with an SS form 7004. Errors cannot be corrected after three years, three months, and 15 days.

Paycheck receipts and year end tax forms from your employer should be kept for IRA verification of taxes, social security, and income.

Accurate home improvement records of property owned should be kept for taxes. The items increase tax base and can reduce capital gains taxes when selling.

Education records such as diplomas, SAT scores, classes and conferences attended, and awards should be kept indefinitely.

Bank records should be kept indefinitely except checks written out for items such as cash and groceries. The source of a deposit written on a deposit slip or bank savings or check book can help trace checks.

Receipts for items such as major purchases, insurance premiums loan payments, and rents should be kept indefinitely. They are important for recovering insurance losses, for problems related to purchases, disagreements, and legal problems. Keep warranties, service contracts, and operating instructions.

Warranties, service contracts, and operating instructions should be sorted each year.

A written or video household inventory should be kept in a safe place that cannot be stolen or burned in a fire. If necessary, make a second copy. The best place is a safety deposit box.

A number list should be made, with a copy in a safe place, of bank account numbers, creditors, insurance agents' telephone numbers, service providers, credit card and insurance policy numbers.:

CONSUMER PROTECTION

Mailboxes fill with advertisements that mislead. Telephones ring with offers to sell and defraud. Even the Internet has dishonest con-artists waiting to get your dollars. You can avoid most of the schemes.

Fraudulent Schemes

"Bait and Switch" techniques offer items at a very low price. When you come to shop, they offer higher priced items and encourage you to buy. (Used especially for automobile sales.)

"Lo-balling" offers a low price for a service or product and then really charges high prices for other services that are included such as parts and labor. They may also entice with a low price, but when it comes to signing a contract, the price is changed.

Deceptive pricing marks merchandise up in price and then marks the merchandise down so the item looks like it's on sale.

Telemarketing fraud is often a scam. Things you can do to protect yourself are:

- Avoid postcard and telephone scams that offer very good deals at very low prices.
- Don't be pressured to buy "NOW" because the prices may rise.
- Never give out your credit card number over the phone.

- Double check travel offers by checking them with the Better Business Bureau. Ask detailed questions about hotels, transportation, and check out the places yourself. (Ask about cancellations and refunds.)
- Get all details in writing.
- **Don't** send money by messenger or overnight mail. **Don't** pay in cash. (You can lose your right to dispute a fraudulent claim if you pay cash. People can also disappear with your funds.)
- **If in doubt, say "No!"**

- Gifts arriving in the mail do not require payment or return. If item is expensive, it is best to let postal authorities know.
- Earn-at-home schemes are often frauds. Materials are sometimes sold to make products. When the work is done, it may be refused as unsatisfactory, but the company benefits from the sale of materials. Be sure to check carefully. These companies often work from post office boxes and are not available for communication.

- Club contracts such as those used for books, records, and tapes may or may not be honest. Companies benefit from customers who don't cancel the next month's offering by returning the refusal form in time. The merchandise will then be sent along with a bill.
- Learn-at-home schooling can also be a fraud. Check with the Better Business Bureau. Then contact a company that might hire you after your training to see if the earned credentials are meaningful.
- Coupon books can be tempting. The merchandize may not be needed or located for easy use.
- Watch out for any "good deal." Watch for products with hype words such as love, beauty, wealth, and admiration. Ask what they are really selling!
- Just because items are advertised in newspapers and magazines doesn't mean that they are legitimate.

CHECK COMPANY REPUTATION!

- Beware of special offers such as one for "a huge beauty kit." Small items can be packaged as huge.
- Chain letters and pyramids are illegal. By the time the chain goes around, millions of people can become involved. The chain breaks so that only the first few people benefit.
- On-the-road-sales-jobs may not allow participants to return home when they wish. High pressure sales encourage joining with promises

of big money. Check the reputation of the company carefully.

- Sweepstake offers are especially misleading. The written information is created to confuse the customer and to get an order. The possibility of winning is like a million-to-one shot and is always noted in very, very small print.
- Be alert for counterfeit products. Big name brands are often copied and sold at a much lower cost than normal.

Complaining About a Product

If you have a complaint about a product, the Federal Trade Commission (FTC) enforces the guarantee. First talk to your local dealer. (Be sure that you followed directions given to you!) Take your sales receipt and warranty. If the problems can't be resolved, contact the manufacturer by mail. Send only copies of the original receipts. Include:

- Your name, address, phone number, account number, serial and model numbers, date, place purchased.
- Explanation of history and facts about the problem explaining whom you contacted and when.
- Copies of documents relating to the problem.
- Specific action of what you would like the company to do (i.e. return money, send new item).
- Date limit of when you expect them to take action allowing enough response time.
- Information on how you can be reached.

If you still receive no satisfaction, contact a radio or TV station that has a consumer advocate dealing with individual consumer problems or get the help of a consumer group. Look in telephone directory under City and County Protection Services or Consumer Groups. or write to:

U.S. Office of Consumer Affairs
Department of Health and Human Services
300 Seventh Street SW
Washington DC 20004

Finally, if all else fails, try legal action through a small claims court.

Starting Out Supplies

"What kind of supplies do I need to start out living on my own?"

When you leave home you leave a whole houseful of supplies. It can come as a surprise when you realize what you'll need when you start out on your own. The following lists of suggestions for dorms or apartments may seem overwhelming. Your choices will depend on what **you** feel is important. A person can start out with one dish, one spoon, one knife, one pan, one blanket, a bar of soap, one towel and then makeshift and borrow for the rest. This can make for a Spartan existence, but it is not impossible.

If you prefer a more comfortable existence, you can begin collecting things at low cost, free of charge, or on loan. You will find that discount stores run specials at the beginning of new school terms. That is a good time to buy some essentials. Relatives may have extra equipment. Check in Goodwill stores, used furniture stores, antique stores, thrift shops, rummage sales, garage sales, and flea markets.

Equipment List For Dorms

If you want to avoid the last minute rush of gathering things, start early. If you wait until you get on campus, you may find that things are more costly and good shopping may be far away in unfamiliar territory. Small stores near the campus generally have higher prices.

First research the college of your choice before you go. You can go to visit the campus and visit dorm rooms to talk with students. If you can't get to the campus, talk with someone near you who goes there. If necessary, find a name and write. Ask "What's in?" on the campus you'll attend. You will find that campuses differ, so don't expect to find answers from someone in a different school. You may be able to find some of this information through a dorm or student housing office. Some helpful things to ask are:

1. What appliances can be used in the room?
2. What "comforts" are available in the dorm such as televisions, microwaves, computers, refrigerators, washing facilities, cooking facilities, irons, ironing boards, sweepers, and linens? What is the cost for use of these "comforts"?
3. What type of clothing is appropriate?

Also try to contact your new roommate to coordinate what each person plans to bring to the room, to avoid duplication of musical equipment, lamps, chairs, and such. It's best to avoid sharing the expense of a large purchase until you know your roommate. You may find you are incompatible. Plans should be considered for disposal of the items when you no longer live together.

Look through all the things that you use each day at home and decide what you are going to need. Plan to take along some favorite things that will make you feel at home...a favorite poster, pictures, pillow, stuffed animal, or model. Include a photo album and pre-addressed and stamped postcards.

DORM CHECK LIST OF EQUIPMENT/SUPPLIES

APPLIANCES

Iron	Hair dryer	Curling iron/curlers
Sandwich maker	Computer	Mirror
Electric shaver	Vaporizer	Popcorn popper
Floor lamps	Desk lamp	Typewriter
Clip-on lamp	Clock/radio	Radio
Music equipment	Phone	Tapes
CDs	Coffee pot	Window fan
Hot pot		

ORGANIZATION AIDS

Plastic containers with dividers	Paper liner for drawers
Hangers	Address book
Shoe rack	Under bed storage containers
Key ring	Camera & Supplies
Account book for spending record	Door memo pad
Financial record box	Bulletin board
Stationery/stamps	Scrapbook/photo albums
Plastic crates/storage	Wall hangers

STUDY AIDS

Thesaurus and dictionary	Ruler
Pencils	Stapler
Study planner	Folders for reports/filing

Paper clips
Glue
Masking/transparent tape
Computer disks
T-square
Lap desk
Compass
Notebooks (See what's used)
Colored pencils
Variety of paper

Thumbtacks
Backpack
Calculator
Markers
Resources you might use
Book ends
Pens
Erasers
Index cards

REPAIR SUPPLIES

Smoke alarm, if not furnished
Thread
Hammer
Safety/straight pins
Scissors
Pliers
Wire for hanging pictures
Tool kit

Needles
Tape measure
Screwdriver
Pin cushion
Sewing kit
Small nails
Buttons

EMERGENCY SUPPLIES

Alcohol swab towelettes
Antacid
Sunscreen
Adhesive tape
Bandaids
Mild antibacterial soap
Needle
Laxative
Flashlight & batteries
Insect repellent
Compression bandage
Eyewash
Antifungal spray
Personal medications
Aspirin or equivalent

Cough syrup/spoon
Rubbing alcohol
Antiseptic first-aid spray
Antidiarrheal
Thermometer
Candles for light failure
Tweezers
Syrup of ipecac (for poisoning)
Safety pins
Ice bag
Emergency numbers
Battery charger
Gauze pads 2x2"& 4x4"
First aid kit/manual
2" gauze pads

CLEANING EQUIPMENT

Laundry basket
Laundry detergent
Stain pretreatment
All-purpose bleach
Measuring cup
Laundry clothes bag
Clothes drying rack (even rope)
Dust cloth or paper
Cleaning tray basket or bucket
Cleaning rags
All-purpose cleaner for surfaces

Small plastic bucket
Whisk broom
Fabric softener
Clothes brush
Waste basket
Shoe polish, brushes
Sponge
Abrasive cleanser
Toothbrush
Window cleaner
Razor blade in safety holder

GROOMING EQUIPMENT

Grooming Bucket to Carry The Following Supplies:

Nail file/emery boards, clippers
Shampoo
Skin lotion

Mouthwash
Deodorant
Plastic covered soap dish

Hair conditioner
Tissues
Soap
Brush
Dental Floss
Mirror
After-shave lotion
Suntan lotion

Toothpaste/toothbrush
Talcum powder
Plastic glass
Blades
Personal grooming cosmetics
Razor
Comb

SNACKING EQUIPMENT

Large bowl (for popcorn!)
Sharp knife
Measuring spoons & cups
Eating utensils
Unbreakable cups, glasses, dishes
Dish towel/cloth
Aluminum foil

Plastic storage containers/lids
Can opener
Bottle opener
Paper towels
Salt/pepper shakers
Plastic bags

SNACK FOOD SUPPLIES

Easily kept, non-refrigerated foods:
Popcorn
Soups
Jellies
Tea bags/instant tea
Hot chocolate

Peanut butter
Crackers
Cereals
Instant coffee

FURNITURE/LINENS/DECORATIONS

Pillows
Towels/washcloths
Bedspread
Extra blanket/sleeping bag
Afghan
Drapes (if not furnished)*
Small rugs
Stackable crates/shelves

Sheets, pads, blankets not furnished
Large rug*
Comforter (can use as spread)
Pictures/posters
Plants (if you like them)
Chairs (if space allows)
Trunk (can use as table or seat)
Throw pillows

* Large rugs can be made by fitting together rug samples
Drapes can be made inexpensively from sheets, or patchwork of varied fabrics sewn together. Shades can also be used.
Check bulletin boards...sometimes students sell their drapes or other items at the end of a semester.

How Much ?!?

Equipment List for Apartments

When preparing to go into an apartment, preplan your needs by checking with people who are living in the area in which you hope to have an apartment. If you are on a campus or in a new community starting a new job, reread the previous section. You can check "what's in" there, too. The following list may be needed in addition to what you want to choose from the dorm room list.

APARTMENT CHECK LIST OF EQUIPMENT & SUPPLIES

KITCHEN SUPPLIES

For Storage

*Aluminum foil
*Garbage bags
Masking tape
Plastic wrap
*Plastic bags
Grease can (i.e. coffee can)
Freezer paper

For Food Preparation

*2-cup liquid measuring cup
*Measuring spoons
*Spatula/pancake turner
*Bottle opener
*Graduated measuring cups
*Mixing bowls
*Salt and pepper shakers
Potato masher
Nutcracker (can use hammer)
Slotted spoon
Tongs
Baster
Pastry brush
Rubber spatula
Ladle
Varied knives
Funnel
Pizza cutter
Kitchen shears

*Can opener
*Vegetable peeler
*Small all metal spatula
*Pot holders
*Paring knife
*Mixing spoon
*Serated knife
Apple corer
Egg beater (can use fork)
Trivets
Corkscrew
Cooking fork
Rolling pin
Timer
Canister set
Cutting board
Serving tray
Wire whisk
Strainer/colander

For Cooking

*2-quart casserole with cover
*Loaf pan
Griddle
*6-quart pot with lid
Pie tins

*Cookie sheet
*Frying pan
*Saucepans 1, 2, 3 quarts with lids
*9x13" cake pan
Muffin tins

Table service

*Dinner plates
*Glasses
*Cups/mugs
Platter

*Silverware
*Cereal bowls
Salad bowl
*Serving dishes

Appliances

*Iron
*Clock radio
Coffee pot
Refrigerator
Electric knife
Toaster
Electric hand mixer
Heating pad
Lighted make-up mirror
Toaster oven
Espresso coffee maker

*Window fan (if no air conditioner)
*Extension cord
*Humidifier/vaporizer (for dry, overheated rooms)
Electric wok
Electric mixer
Electric frying pan
Food processor
Hair dryer
Typewriter/computer
Popcorn popper

Food Staples

Coffee, tea, chocolate
Cereals
Soy Sauce
Vanilla
Salt
Garlic salt
Pepper
Thyme
Sage
Oil
Pasta
Dry soups
Brown/white/confectioners' sugar
Onion flakes

Baking soda
Hot sauce
Basil
Vinegar
Oregano
Paprika
Flour
Baking powder
Rice
Cornstarch
Cocoa
Cinnamon
Shortening

GENERAL SUPPLIES

*Ironing board
*Covered wastebasket
Light bulbs

*Wastebasket
*Buckets
*Recycling bin

BATHROOM SUPPLIES

*Bar soap
*Shower curtains (if no door)
*Soap dish that drains
*Shower rings (if use curtain)
*Glasses/cup
*Toilet paper
*Tissues
*Personal toiletries
*Dental floss
*Hair brush/comb
Mats for floor and tub
Handheld shower extension

*Shampoo
Shower caddy
*Towels (2 large, 2 hand, cloths)
Electric razor
*Toilet brush
Heating Pad
*Toothpaste
Icebag
*First aid kit (see above in Dorm)
Wastebasket
Toothbrush holder
Hamper

BEDROOM SUPPLIES

*2 sets of sheets/pillow cases
*2 or 3 blankets
*Comforter (can serve as spread)
*Bedside lamp

*Pillow
*Alarm/radio
*Mattress pad

TOOLS FOR REPAIRS

*2 Phillips head screwdrivers (sized #1 and #2)
*4-in-1 screwdriver (1/8", 1/4", 5/16", 3/8")
*Crescent adjustable 10" wrench
*Slip-joint pliers with wire cutter jaws
Electric drill
*13-oz claw hammer with magnetized end
24-26" crosscut steel blade handsaw (7-8pts/in)

Plunger	Nail and screw assortment
Work gloves	Work goggles
Drop cord	6 ft retractable steel tape
All-purpose oil	Long nose pliers
Masking tape	White glue
Sandpaper	Electric tape
Voltage tester	Stud finder
Retractable utility knife	Heavy-duty staple gun
Step stool	

CLEANING PRODUCTS

(See "Getting Cleaned Up For Company" on page 94 for further information.)

All-purpose cleaner	Drain cleaner
Toilet bowl cleaner	White vinegar
Carpet cleaner	Glass cleaner
Tub, tile, sink cleanser	Broom/dustpan
Insecticides	Furniture polish
Oven cleaner	Hand-held vacuum
Disinfectant	Metal cleaner
Wax for floors	Vacuum
Ammonia	Bleach
Detergent	Mop, dry and wet
Sponges	Rags
Bucket	Baking soda

*These items are considered essential. All others are "nice-to-haves."

SUPPLIES LISTED IN DORM ROOM

Refer to "Dorm Check List of Equipment/Supplies"

Guidelines for Buying Secondhand Appliances

There is so much to buy as you begin on your own. One possibility of saving dollars is to purchase used appliances. There can be excellent buys and there can be poor ones. There will be some risk involved. Ways to protect yourself are:

- Research *Consumer Reports.*
- Question repairmen (a quick telephone call helps).
- Look for UL safety seal, sound cord, plug and wiring insulation.
- See that parts and finish are in sound condition with no signs of rust or deterioration.
- Look for indications of good care and cleanliness.
- Plug it in to see if it works.

Places to Purchase

Private Families

Classified newspaper ads offer information of where to purchase. Question by phone first of all. Find the age and condition of the appliance. If you go to see it, take someone with you for safety and advice. You will probably have to transport the piece yourself, so take that into consideration. Try it out to see that it works.

Appliance and Repair Stores

Sometimes trade-ins are taken in stores that sell appliances. They may be cleaned up and repaired. They may also be sold to repair stores for resale. There are often limited guarantees with the products, such as for 90 days on parts and labor. If sold as "rebuilt", there are more extensive repairs and renovation. Check the reputation of the stores before purchase.

Outlets, Garage Sales, Auctions, Moving Companies

Donations, unclaimed, or salvaged appliances can be very good buys. Check equipment before buying and ask for any refund privilege in writing. If purchasing at an auction, check condition of appliance before bidding begins to avoid "auction fever".

Furnishing with Old and New

"How do I put my 'stuff' together and make it right for me?"

Castoffs and treasures from attics to curbsides can make attractive furnishings for your new living space. They may not look like they fit together, but time and imagination can create miracles! You may even be able to purchase some new things. Put them all together with your own values, style, personality, lifestyle, and budget.

Consider What Your Decorating Needs Are

Your Values?

What value do you put on decorating your space? Is it a waste of time? Do friends or family care?

Your Style?

What do you want your space to look like? Dramatic? Formal? Comfortable? Trendy? Modern?

Your Personality?

What do you want people to know about you when they enter your space? Are there personal things that show your interests such as a painting, a hobby, a piece of antique furniture? Do you like things neat? Cheery? Quiet? Intellectual? Lived-in?

Your Lifestyle?

What kind of lifestyle will you lead? Will you entertain often? How will you entertain? Do you want quiet for studying and reading? Do you want things organized for little cleaning? Do you need space and equipment for a hobby?

Your Budget?

How much money can you spend on decorating and furnishing? Can you do it all at once? Do you want to use what you purchase later in your life? Do you want to sell or leave things behind when you move?

Create a Decorating Plan
#1 Study Decorating Ideas

If you find that you would like your living space to "look good," find information and make a plan. The library is a good resource. Look at pictures in decorating magazines to develop an "eye" for decorating and discover your likes and dislikes.

#2 Choose a Style and Theme

Styles of furnishings vary. *Cottage* is casual, comfortable, and cluttered, using natural materials, small design fabrics, and simple furniture. *Country* is similar, but more luxurious. *Town House* is dramatic, elegant, and refined, using shiny metals, glass, and rich carpets. *International* is expensive, elegant, and very formal, using modern furniture, rugs over carpets, and built-ins. *Minimal* is uncluttered, intellectual, and simple, using plain textured fabrics, neutral walls, and built-ins. *Eclectic* is creative and personal, using anything!

Young adults just starting out often choose **eclectic**. This style builds on a theme to carry out their own personality and creativity by using whatever they have or gather. Success depends on careful planning of color and furniture grouping so things tie together and appear uncluttered. A room is centered on one object. The colors of the item carry out the theme through walls and furnishings or a neutral background draws attention to the item.

Suggested theme ideas:

Grandma's Attic (antiques, old handwork, quilt, family pictures, "junk," old clothes, collage of "old things," dishes, old pots and containers...most anything)

Airplanes (models, parachute, posters, airplane pictures, maps)

Automobiles (models, old auto seats, posters, tools, road maps)

Garden (plants, outdoor furniture, picnic baskets, checked tablecloths)

Library (books, computer, collage of computer disks and program covers)

Jungle or cats (stuffed animals, pictures, white fur spread, zebra or leopard fabrics)

Country (old patchwork blanket, handwork, handmade articles, baskets, antiques)

Modern, plastic (plastic furniture and milk cartons, straight lines and bright colors)

Sports (sports equipment, posters, baseball card collage, bicycle, stadium blanket, seat cushions, programs, sport clothes)

Music (old or new musical instruments, drum table, record collage, posters, sheet music, handmade instruments like you made as a child, cut-out musical symbols such as notes, clef signs, flats, sharps)

Sewing (sewing machine, collage of sewing equipment, large knitting spools, handmade articles, draped dummy, fabric bolts, fabrics, partially knitted item hung with knitting needles)

Oriental (parasols, fans, Bonsai tree, kimono, plants, paper shades and room dividers, pictures, posters, old oriental rugs)

#3 Use Basic Art Principles

Art principles were taught in art classes during your school days. Here is the place to use them.

Line can make things appear to be what they are not. When any line becomes dominant because of where it is placed or because of its color, your eye will follow this line. This principle of "the eye follows the line" can make things appear larger or smaller. *Horizontal lines* cause the eye to follow it sideways to make an object appear wider. *Vertical lines* cause the eye to move up and down to make an object appear taller.

Color creates atmosphere and affects mood and room size. Yellow, orange, and red give a feeling of warmth and activity and make a room look smaller. Blue and green are restful and relaxing and make a room appear larger. Pale and dull colors give an illusion of space. Bright colors make a room appear smaller. Color accents in furniture and accessories can draw the eye where you want attention and draw a room together. More than three colors can cause confusion.

Balance relates to equilibrium. If things aren't balanced, you feel as if something's wrong, like a teeter-totter with different weights on each end. Balance large and small furniture by keeping the pieces separate from each other. Make small pieces appear larger with addition of accessories, such as lamps, pictures, plants, folding screens, or a coat rack. To emphasize a piece of furniture, use contrasting colors or fabric around it. To camouflage furniture, paint the walls and the furniture similar colors.

Proportion refers to one part of a whole. Large furniture looks best in large rooms. Small furniture looks best in small rooms. Pieces of furniture should create a pleasing relationship between their parts.

#4 Create an Inventory to Help You Plan

After you've gathered your ideas, take an inventory of what you have and what you need.

FURNISHINGS INVENTORY AND PREPLANNING

Decorating Style Preferred (circle)

Cottage/Farmhouse   Country   Town House   International   Minimal   Eclectic

Color preference _____

Size of room(s) #1_____ #2_____ #3_____ #4_____

How I'll use the room(s) (i.e. study, entertain, sleep, hobby)
#1_____
#2_____
#3_____
#4_____

Furnishings I Have

Furnishing	Color	Size	Repair needed	Cost

Appliances I Have

Appliance	Color	Repair needed	Cost

Accessories I Have

Accessory	Color	Repair needed	Cost

Equipment I Have

Equipment	Color	Repair needed	Cost

Furnishings I Need

Furniture	Color	Date needed	Cost

Appliances I Need

Appliances	Date needed	Cost

Accessories I Need

Accessories	Date needed	Cost

Equipment I Need

Accessories	Date needed	Cost

HOW TO PLAN TO MAKE THINGS FIT IN THE ROOMS

If you want to make sure that the furniture you gather will fit in the space that you have, make a floor plan by drawing a room to scale with 1/4"=1" graph paper. Then create exact size furniture templates using outside measurements. Move them around to see how they fit. Allow at least 24" between groupings of furniture, 10" between sofa and coffee table, 18" for pulling out chairs from tables in seating areas.

#5 Comparison Shop

For buying things you still need, shop economically and buy the best quality you can afford.

Relatives and friends may have things to give, sell, or loan.

Auctions sell items "as is." Arrive early to examine merchandise. Register if you really want to buy. Note dents, scratches, etc. Measure to see if items fit. Write down decisions and amount you can pay. You may need cash. Check ahead of time.

Used furniture and furniture rental stores can offer low prices. Compare with cost of new items. Check items carefully. Consider rentals only if your stay is going to be short in an area. Renting with the option to buy is usually costly.

Garage sales have the best bargains. Offer what you think is a fair price. Shop early and move on so you won't miss bargains elsewhere. There are usually no returns allowed.

Flea markets, and pawn shops, offer bargains with no returns. Beware of stolen merchandise.

Antique shops vary in prices. Comparative shop. Bargaining is acceptable.

Department, furniture, and appliance stores can be dependable if you can afford new things. Sales offer competitive prices. Decorating services may be available free of charge.

Factory outlets may cost more than regular store sale prices. Choices can be limited. Check for flaws.

Mail orders can offer unusual and bargain merchandise. Order early enough to receive it. Figure in the delivery charges and return costs. If item arrives too late to use, refuse delivery. Returns should have no charge. Keep all papers relating to purchase.

LOOK WHAT I FOUND!

Television and Internet shopping are convenient. Compare costs with comparable purchases. It's hard to judge quality unseen.

Newspaper want ads, radio programs, and bulletin boards offer bargains. Make telephone calls to check prices, condition, and delivery. If you must go to a house to pick up an item, take someone with you for safety and for help.

Garbage pick-up day offers free bargains right on the street. City dumps may be good too. Call the city and ask about process.

Mission and secondhand stores may have good bargains for housewares and furniture. Check the prices against purchasing new. There is usually a no-return policy.

Hardware stores carry inexpensive, durable furnishings. Explore them. Even call and ask.

> **Warning! Overstuffed furniture may harbor fleas or other "pests."**

USE CREATIVE MONEY-SAVING IDEAS FOR FUTURE OR SHORT TERM

- Buy lawn furniture for kitchen, dining, or living rooms to use later on a patio.
- Consider sturdy, inexpensive plastic furniture available in discount stores.
- Buy a bridge table and chairs to use later.
- Consider antiques or second hand furniture. (Refinish or cover scratches with scratch cover polish.)

- Use pillows for extra chairs or a trunk for a coffee table or chair.
- Use bed alternatives of mattress on floor, sleeping bag, hammock, cot, foam pad, cushions from old couches, fold out couch, flat springs on wooden legs (screw them in), futons.
- Remodel lamps by recovering the shade's frame or adding a new shade.
- Make curtains of old or new bedspreads, tablecloths, valances, sheets. Cover roller blinds with fabric.

USE CREATIVE STORAGE SPACE EQUIPMENT

- Use underbed storage boxes.
- Store extra blankets under a mattress.
- Stack paper file boxes or plastic milk crates to store papers, magazines, and many other things.
- Use small plastic ice cream buckets to hold cosmetics, cleaning supplies, etc.
- Cover cardboard boxes of the same size with contact paper.
- Store belts, mittens, and "whatevers" in pocketed shoe bags.
- Make a shoe rack with a tension rod 4" from the back wall and 6" from the floor of your closet.
- Extend storage space for clothes with an overdoor rack.
- Make shelves with boards and cement blocks or bricks.
- Make a desk by placing a flat door over a pair of two drawer files.

#6 Buy Furnishings Wisely

Judging Quality in Furniture

The choice of furniture depends on its use and length of time it will be used. If you want to buy a piece to keep, judge its quality. You can use the following information to purchase new or old furniture. When making choice of old or new, remember old and antique furniture retain value, but new loses value.

WOODEN FURNITURE (CASE GOODS)

Types of Wood

Wooden furniture (case goods) includes many products such as beds and desks. It can be judged by wood type, finish, and construction features. Ready-to-finish wood furniture is less expensive than finished furniture. It must have a finish applied and some sanding is necessary.

Softwoods come from evergreen trees such as pine. They are generally less expensive than hardwoods, have less grain, and dent easily.

Hardwoods come from trees that produce leaves such as oak, walnut, and mahogany. They are known for grain and durability.

Veneer is a wood "sandwich" of three, five, or seven layers, glued together over a center core of solid lumber. More expensive wood is layered on the outside. Veneers are durable and less expensive than solid wood. Old veneers may need regluing.

Construction of furniture varies. Furniture is as strong as the joints holding it together. Just nails and glue don't last. A combination of sturdy joining processes plus adhesive is best.

Mortise and Tenon fits notches together by fitting a solid piece into a hole in an adjoining piece of wood. No nails or screws are used.

Double Dowel uses wooden pins that are fitted into holes drilled into both adjoining pieces of wood. These are glued together.

Corner blocks are triangular pieces of wood, screwed and glued to support and reinforce frame.

Dovetail joins boards at right angles (as in drawers) by interlocking tenons cut in the form of a dove tail.

Tongue and groove joints are almost invisible. One board has a projecting tongue that fits into a groove in a corresponding board.

Butt joint only glues or nails flush to another board. This is the least desirable of all joints.

CHECKLIST FOR WOOD FURNITURE SHOPPING

- Drawers glide easily and freely on ball bearings or guides
- Drawers don't wobble when opened or closed
- Doors shut tightly without sticking
- Doors are shut with magnetic catches (indicate quality)
- Legs stand squarely on floor
- Corner blocks have been used for reinforcement at corners
- Legs are attached with mortise and tenon or dowel joints
- Dovetail construction is used in drawers
- There are dust panels between drawers (quality furniture)
- Insides of drawers, backs of chests, undersides of tables & chairs sanded & finished
- Surfaces are free from defects, when viewed in good light and touched with fingertips
- A protective coating has been used on tabletops or furniture that has hard wear
- Hardware is of good quality and is fastened securely

UPHOLSTERED FURNITURE

Upholstered furniture is judged for comfort, style, and quality construction. Since you can't see inside of furniture, talk to a salesperson in a store with a good reputation. Read labels and hang tags carefully. Sit in the furniture to see if it fits you. Pillows help if you are short.

Framework of furniture should be made of kiln-dried hardwood. Joints should be securely doweled or mortised, braced, and glued.

Seat Construction supports cushioning materials. *Serpentine or S-type* are most often used today. *Flat S-type* are fastened to the frame with nails and are used when minimum bulk is used. *Coil* springs are attached to webbing or steel bands. There should be 9-12 tied springs in an average-sized chair. Quality furniture has springs tied eight times, less expensive pieces only four times. Ask for information.

Cushioning material covers construction before outer cover is added. Labels describing cushioning materials are attached to muslin dust cover under cushions. Quality furniture uses matched fabric. *Cellular foam* (urethane or polyfoam) is used on arms, back, and seat. It is: durable and lightweight; nonallergenic, mildew, fungus and mothproof; resilient; strong. *Foam*

Mortise and Tenon

Double Dowel

Corner blocks

Dovetail

Tongue and groove

rubber is sometimes used. It is resilient and firm but disintegrates over time. *Latex foam rubber* is very resilient, comfortable for sitting, and more expensive. *Urethane foam* is used as the core of a seat and wrapped with a soft polyester material or down. The foam feels like the luxury of down, but is more resilient and holds its shape.

Outer coverings make an impression of the quality of the furniture. There are different grades used by companies. Check grading quality system used. (Fiber may not be durable, but quality may be high.) Outer covering should be appropriate and durable for its use. Light "chic" fabrics are not as durable and require maintenance unless covered. Look for good fit, good tailoring with smooth straight welting on major seam constructions, zipper closures on cushions that are reversible, straight hanging hems and pleats, and matching patterns where seams meet. Consider ease of cleaning and durability. **Read labels.**

Characteristics of fibers differ. *Rayon* is soft, weak, and is difficult to clean. *Nylon* is easy to clean, strong, and resists abrasion. *Olefins* and *polyesters* are strong, abrasion resistant, mildew and mothproof, are easily washed and spot-cleaned. *Cotton* and *linen*, if woven into high quality fabric, are reasonably durable, but hard to clean if not treated. *Silk* is luxurious, but weak. *Treated fabrics* can have stain and soil resistant finishes like Scotchguard or Teflon.

CHECKLIST FOR BUYING UPHOLSTERED FURNITURE

Frame is kiln-dried
Legs and joints are securely attached
Verified quality of inside of furniture and cushioning materials with salesperson
Can feel webbing holding springs when feeling under the furniture
Webbing under furniture feels wide, closely woven with no gaps (unless steel)
No lumps or bumps
Can't feel framework through upholstery
Cushions fit snugly and evenly against each other
Cushions are zippered, reversible, and interchangeable
Seams are well-stitched
Buttons are hand sewn through the filling, not tacked on
Bottom of furniture is covered with a dust cover
Fabric pattern is matched at visible seams
Outer cover is well-tailored with cording that is not wavy
Fabric of cover is durable with stain-resistant finish on outer fabric
If fabric is stapled, staples are well-hidden under welt cord
Cost is within planned budget
Style and color are appropriate for purpose
Recliners do not jerk when position is moved
Have checked for flammability
Sleeper sofa is comfortable for sitting as well as sleeping

CARPETS/RUGS

Carpets are usually furnished in dorm rooms or apartments. If the color doesn't blend with what you own, cover with blending area or throw rugs. You may choose to buy new. If you choose to buy wall-to-wall carpeting, you must leave it when you move if it is glued or tacked with staples.

How to Choose Carpeting

Textures:
- Tight twist or loop last longest with hard wear.
- Low piles take less cleaning.
- All loops of different heights require more cleaning.

Fibers:
- Wool requires special care, spots more easily, and is not insect-proof.
- Nylon, polyester, olefin, acrylics are resilient, soil resistant, and long-lasting.
- Cotton and rayon may be less costly, but are not as durable. Rayon is the least durable.
- The more dense the fibers (with tufts closely packed together), the longer they will wear.

Construction and Quality:
- Carpets are woven, tufted, or knitted.
- Carpets are graded. Judge quality by the fiber and thickness of the fibers. There should be little space when fibers are spread with fingers.
- *Backing* that holds the carpet together prevents buckling, stretching, and shrinking, is usually made of latex. Good quality has an extra layer. Some have no backing.
- *Padding* (underlay or cushion) absorbs shocks, extends rug life, and adds depth of feel to the carpet. It is made of felt, rubber, or synthetics and can be textured for buoyancy.

MATTRESSES

Research name brand companies when buying a mattress. Watch for sales. Buy the finest quality you can afford so that it will last longer. Buying used mattresses can offer problems.

Mattresses are made of different shapes of springs joined together. Quality is judged by the steel in the springs, the method holding them together, and the fabric layering used. Depend on salesperson for information.

Box springs are built like mattresses except insulator and cushioning materials are omitted. Coils are braced from frames and slats fastened at intervals along the bottom. Wood used should be kiln dried. Some box springs have no coverings. It's best to match mattress and box spring.

Foundations are boards in the shape of a box spring. They look the same from the outside, but are not long lasting. They are sold in less expensive mattress and box spring sets.

Waterbeds come in varying quality. The water-filled mattress is contained in a box. It requires filling with water and needs to be emptied before moving or treating for mold. Before deciding to buy, consider the extra costs and effort involved: cost of heating, special sheets, insurance for water damage. Test to see if bed is comfortable and if getting in and out of bed is difficult.

Futons are couches that can be used as beds. They are inexpensive.

Bed frames hold mattresses. They can be used separately or attached to headboards.

MATTRESS BUYING CHECK LIST

Investigated name brand mattress
Talked to salesperson about quality
Comfortable...tried it out by rolling over on it several times
Good resiliency
Steel of coils is strong and thick
Coils are put together for long lasting use and strength
Cost fits my budget
Cover is good quality
Boxspring is built of kiln-dried wood of good quality
Boxspring rows of coils are separated by wooden slats
Boxspring is of equal quality of mattress

LINENS

Cotton and blends are used for sheets, table coverings, and towels, but the term "linens" stays with us.

Sheets/pillow cases

Size of sheets is printed on label and packaging. There are sizes for single, double, queen, and king beds. There are also sizes for cribs, cots, youth, daybeds, foam mattresses, and extra long. (These sheets are usually more expensive and not as easy to find.) Fitted sheets are sewn to hug the mattress. Usual sizes

for flat sheets in inches:

- *Single* 63x108
- *Double* 81x108 or 90x108
- *Queen* 90x120
- *King* 100x120 or 108x120.

Standard sheets and blankets may not fit since mattresses vary in size. Foam mattresses are about 4 inches thick and innerspring mattresses are about 6 inches. Carry measurements of your mattress with you and check against the measurements on the linens. Allow for tuck-in at the bottom of flat sheets and a tuck-over at the top to protect the edge of blankets. Check fitted sheets for strong, taped seams.

Sheets are usually a cotton and polyester blend or 100% cotton. Judge fabric by number of threads per square inch. The higher the number, the more costly the sheet. Percale has 180 to 200 threads per square inch, is more expensive, lightweight, smooth, and durable. Muslin has 112 to 140 threads per square inch, costs less, and is rougher to the touch. The 112 muslin is very poor quality, 128 is fair, and 140 is excellent. Sheets may be sized with starch to make them appear heavier. Customer is fooled into thinking quality is higher. Check for starch sizing by rubbing corners together to see if they become thinner. If sheets or pillowcases are not sanforized or preshrunk, recognize that they may shrink. If possible buy them 2% longer. (Read the label.) Purchase pillow cases longer than pillows they cover. Sizes are regular, queen, and king. For width, measure the pillow, double the amount and add 2 or 3 inches.

BLANKETS

Deep fluffy napped blankets are warmer than tightly woven ones. Nap allows air to become trapped for warmth. Blankets are made of various fabrics.

- **Wool** is considered very warm. It is not mothproof. Most require dry-cleaning. (See label.)
- **Acrylic** is as warm as wool of comparable construction but is not as springy. It creates static electricity, pills, wrinkles, is mothproof and allergy free, can be washed with care, and is low in cost.
- **Cotton** is used for warmer weather since it doesn't have characteristics that create warmth. It is easy to care for and is mothproof.

- **Down** is warm and light. It is available in comforters that can act as a spread as well as a blanket. Down needs to be fluffed. It is best not to clean it often, so a cover over the comforter is used.
- **Rayon** is more expensive and gets shaggy when washed. Treated rayon is more durable.
- **Thermal** blankets are made of loosely woven waffle-weave synthetic fabrics, cotton, or wool. These can be used year-round. Used as lightweight cover in summer and with spread on top in winter.
- **Electric** blankets add warmth without weight. They are generally made of synthetic fibers. A UL seal of approval should be on label with latest information on safety of these blankets.

PILLOWS

Fillings for pillows are: down, feathers, fiberfill, rubber, foam. One-piece foams are most durable when compared to shredded or clumps of foam. Rubber foam deteriorates. Fiberfills and foams are non-allergenic and mothproof. Choose what's comfortable. Buy firmly woven covers sewn with welt seams.

TOWELS

Terry cloth is used in bath towels because it's absorbent and durable. Hold towels up to the light to see they are tightly woven. White towels are the most absorbent. Colored towels sometimes bleed and can't be bleached. Terry cloth or woven fabrics are used for kitchen towels. Printed towels are not as absorbent or durable. 100% cotton are more absorbent than blends or synthetics. Choose a fabric for dishes that leaves no lint.

APPLIANCES

If you are buying new appliances, check *Consumer Reports* at the library or through your computer. Buy a recognized appliance brand. Choose a dealer you know and trust so returns and repairs are easier. Make sure that a reliable service is available. Consider repair costs, warranty, apartment's wiring capacity, water pressure and space. Also consider buying secondhand. Know cost of running appliance. (New refrigerators are required to have a visible **energy guide label** on the outside that tells the cost of running the appliance. The label allows comparisons. Energy-saving appliances may cost more, but can save enough to pay the difference.) If you are on a limited budget, you will find a standard model is the best buy. Upgraded models offer more features which add to cost and need for repair.

WINDOW COVERINGS

There are many types of window coverings:

Glass curtains: transparent or translucent glass fabric in simple, straight lines. Often used under drapes.

Sash curtains: similar to glass curtains; shirred over rods at top and bottom.

Cafe curtains: hung from cafe rod with loops, rings, or clips. May be used alone or in tiers with or without other curtains.

Draw curtains: made from sheer fabric. Hang on traverse rod so they can open and close.

Casement curtains: only reach sill of window. Fabrics are opaque and seldom lined. Hang on traverse rods so they open and close.

Draw draperies: heavier materials than draw curtains. Use traverse rods to open and close.

Tie back curtains: often ruffled, hanging from straight rod. Panels are tied back and held to frame of wall by loops of fabric or special fixtures.

Crisscross or Priscilla curtains: ruffled, extra wide panels mounted so they overlap and then tie back.

Headings: hang at top of window to decorate it. They take the form of:

Valance: may be gathered in some form and often stiffened with a heavy fabric.

Swag: draped piece of fabric sometimes extending down side.

Cornice: stiff boxlike frame that is painted or covered with fabric.

Roller shades: plastic, bamboo, or fabric roll-up on a roller that has a spring to assist rolling.

Austrian: shirrs and drapes when raised or lowered. Pulled up with cord, rings, and pulley.

Roman shades: lie in flat pleats when drawn up with cord, rings, and pulleys.

Venetian blinds: made of wood, plastic, or metal slats held together with tapes and cords.

Vertical blinds: similar to Venetian blinds, but

control light from side to side with vertical slats.

Bamboo or split reed shades: hang horizontally or vertically. They roll up with cords attached.

Wooden shutters: have adjustable louvers. They come in many colors and finishes.

How To Measure for Drapes or Shades

Each type of window treatment requires some method of hanging. You will have to measure to figure the size of the curtain, shade, and rod. Carry accurate measurements with you when buying curtains, rods or shades. **Rounding off to the nearest number just won't work.**

You will need to decide how long you want the curtain or drapery to be. If you have questions, ask the clerk. Remember that if you use draw draperies, inches need to be added for covering the rod from the wall and an overlap that keeps curtain closed well. Check to see if the drapery has allowance for this extra material needed.

HOW TO MEASURE

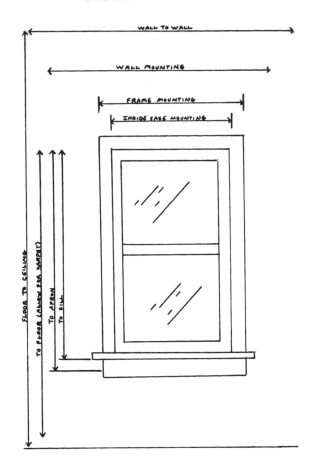

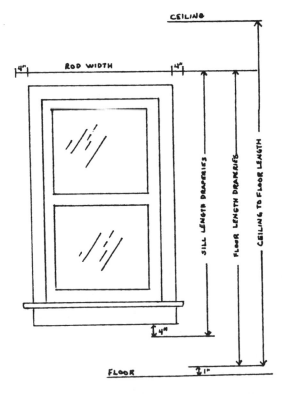

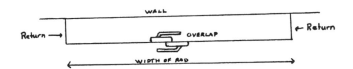

Finding My Own Place

"How can I find a place to live that I like and can afford?"

Needs vs. Wants

We often fall prey to what we WANT rather than what we really NEED. Since we can't afford everything we want, compromises must be made. This takes some soul searching. You'll want to consider: what you can afford; where you want to live; what kind of space you need for your lifestyle.

CHECKLIST FOR WANTS AND NEEDS

COST	LOCATION	SPACE/LIFESTYLE
Fits budget	Near transportation	Appropriate number of bedrooms
Heat furnished	Near shopping	Central heating
Furniture furnished	Near family/friends	In "good" location
Refrigerator furnished	Safe area and security	Yard
Dishwasher/garbage disposal furnished	Close to laundromat	Balcony
Laundry equipment furnished	View from windows	Enough dry & clean storage
Electric or gas range furnished	Near appropriate church	Dining area
All yard/sidewalk services provided	Near recreation	Swimming pool
Window coverings furnished	Parking available for self & guests	Meeting/party room available
Garage at no cost	Quiet	Caretaker on premises
Air conditioner furnished	Near school/campus/ education	Pets allowed
No decorating needed	Near library	"Elegant" decorating

What Are My Housing Alternatives?

Apartment Rental units that are available in various sizes, usually with one, two or three bedrooms. There are single apartments in private homes or varying numbers in buildings or sets of buildings.

Condominiums Apartment units are owned by the people living in them. The owners sell, rent, or use them. In addition to the apartment unit, areas such as hallways, elevators, yards, garages, parking, elevators, and recreational areas are owned with other owners. Maintenance fees are charged to maintain the common areas of the condominium complex.

Cooperatives Apartment units are owned cooperatively as a share of a corporation. They are controlled by a board of directors. Each member has one vote and pays a proportionate share of all costs. A committee approves applicants.

Duplex A duplex includes two apartments that are like two separate houses, located side by side.

Efficiency Apartment Has only one room which includes a cooking area, private bath.

Fraternity/Sorority House Large house usually found on college/university campuses. They generally include food service programs. Most have shared rooms, bathrooms, and recreational areas. Contract termination and refunds are limited. A person must receive an invitation to live in the house.

Garden Apartments Apartment that is usually on the ground level with a yard and garden available.

High-rise or Tower Apartments Apartments located in tall buildings.

House Single housing units surrounded by yard. There are varying sizes.

Mobile Home Housing (manufactured housing) is built in a factory and transported to a community park or private plot of land. They offer more privacy than apartments since they usually include a yard.

Pool Apartments Apartments that have a pool available.

Rooms Private rooms, sometimes including a bathroom, are found in private homes, apartment buildings, rooming houses, YMCA, YWCA, hotels, and motels. Services vary in privacy, food plans, and facilities.

Residence Halls Usually found on college/university campuses. They generally include food service programs. Most have shared rooms, bathrooms, and recreational areas. Contract termination and refunds are limited.

Studio Apartments Usually one room with a separate kitchen and private bath.

Town house Two or more apartments that are like separate houses, connected by common walls, usually in rows.

How Can I Find an Apartment?

- Read newspaper classified ads. Get directly from newspaper office as soon as possible!
- Let friends, relatives, colleagues, and work personnel help. Check with merchants (also their bulletin boards) in grocery stores, local colleges, churches, and laundries in the neighborhood you've chosen.
- Check front door lobbies or signs on apartment buildings in the neighborhood.
- Ask at the local chamber of commerce and at local churches.
- Ask in personnel office where you work or in the housing office at schools.
- Use a fee-charging rental referral agency. Check first with the Better Business Bureau for complaints. (Often rental-referral agencies only use newspaper ads and telephone to apartment complexes. You can do this yourself for NO cost!)
- Call offices of apartment management, property management, and real estate firms. Use Yellow Pages under "Apartment Rentals."

How Do I Approach the Landlord?

You are entering a world where the buyer must beware. When signing a lease, you are signing a contract to pay someone $2,000-3,000 a year. **Be careful, but don't be afraid!** You have the right as a consumer to honest answers and to written agreements. Remember that the person from whom you rent today, may not be there when you leave. Agreements are quickly forgotten, so get **everything in writing**. A person who is unwilling to sign agreements probably will not be the kind of landlord that you want.

Put your best foot forward. The landlord is inspecting you as you inspect the apartment. Use courtesy and tact. Be persistent. Be neat, pleasant, and cooperative. Be prepared with information the landlord may want such as credit and personal references and employment history.

How Do I Fill Out Application Forms?

Many landlords ask to have an application form filled out and some require a fee. Usually if you are accepted, a landlord will hold the apartment for you while checking your credit, employer, and references. Be sure to ask if you will get your application fee back. Local laws don't always require the landlord to refund an application fee unless the applicant is rejected. You should be protected in writing, stating how you will have the fee refunded or applied to your first month's rent. Check to see:

- What happens if the rental unit can't be provided for any reason.
- How long it will take the landlord to notify you of your acceptance or rejection.
- If you must rent the unit if you are accepted.
- That you are being shown the actual rental unit you will be renting, not one "just like it."

There are laws that state you can't be denied housing by a landlord on the basis of color, religion, sex, or national origin. The law applies to all multifamily dwellings except for housing with four or fewer units if the owner is residing in the same complex.

What Should I Look For in an Apartment?

Don't jump at the first apartment you see! Shop around as you would for any purchase you make. This is probably going to take at least one-fourth of your income...one of your biggest expenses. Often the housing you can afford when you start out on your own may be older and less than what you would prefer. Be sure that you choose the best that you can.

Inspect the housing before you make an agreement. Look at the exact unit you will rent. It's best to see it during the day and at night if you can.

The unit should be in "habitable" condition before you move in. Some unhealthy, unsafe living conditions are against housing codes such as: windows broken or painted shut; inadequate heat; doors or windows that don't lock; bad plumbing; cluttered hallways; rats, roaches, mice; bad odors and mold; leaking roofs; lead based paint. You can check with the government office that enforces the codes. If you still want to rent an apartment that doesn't have "habitable" conditions because it is all that you can afford, put in writing how and when the conditions will be corrected. All of these things should be done BEFORE you move in. Do consider that a landlord who allows these conditions to exist in the first place, may not be the best choice for you.

CHECK WITH THE NEIGHBORS

Talk to some of the renters by knocking on their doors, waiting in the entry to question them, or taking names from mailboxes and calling. You could ask such questions as: How quickly are repairs made? Do they know whom to contact if there's a problem? Is there enough heat, hot water, and water pressure? What problems are there in renting there?

INSPECT THE APARTMENT CAREFULLY!

Checking and comparing apartments can save you many frustrations and disagreements with your landlord. When you check the apartment you should look at everything. If you don't, you could end up mid-shower with no hot water or water pressure, windows that won't open for cross ventilation, one outlet per room, or poor lighting. You could swelter in an apartment with windows that are painted shut or fight with hordes of gnats or mosquitoes because there are no screens.

The following "Apartment Inspection Check List" may seem picky as you read it, but if you don't take it seriously, you can end up dollars short, injured, angry, and uncomfortable.

APARTMENT INSPECTION CHECK LIST

Address _____ Apartment # _____

Name of landlord or representative _____

Telephone number of landlord or representative _____

Rent	Deposits	Extra fees	Rugs included
Appliances included		Drapes included	
Utilities available: Gas	Electricity	Paid by:	
Type of heat	Paid by:	Average Cost per Month	
Cable hook-up included		Air-conditioning included	
Pets allowed		Subleasing allowed	

Rental terms _____

House rules _____

_____

_____

What should be done by landlord before moving in (i.e. painting) _____

_____

Number of rooms _____ Numbers of bedrooms _____

INSIDE SPACE INVENTORY	SAFETY INVENTORY
Kitchen:	**Doors, windows, exits:**
Refrigerator works, shelves all there	Dead bolt locks on all doors
All burners work on the range	Through-the-door viewing aperture
Garbage disposal works	Outside doors and windows lock with adequate locks
Sufficient electrical outlets for appliances	At least two exits in case of fire
Hot and cold water pressure sufficient	Fire escapes in good repair
Bathroom:	**Entries, parking lots:**
Toilet flushes	Parking area, stairways, and halls well lit
Sufficient water pressure for hot and cold water	Trash collected regularly
No leaky faucets (check under sink and toilet)	Railings, balcony, walls, steps in good repair
Sufficient ventilation	Laundry facility safe
Tub/shower in good condition	Main floor windows have "stop-blocks"
Bedrooms:	**SERVICES INVENTORY**
Enough closet space	Building management reliable
Appropriate electrical outlets	Garage well lit and maintained
Sufficient size for bed and furniture	Recreational facilities and yard well maintained
Waterbeds allowed	Rodents and roaches under control

What Do I Need to Know About Rental Agreements?

NO LEASE (Tenancy at Will)

A lease is sometimes called "a tenancy at will" since no written agreement is made. Disadvantages of this agreement are: the lease is renewed automatically every month; the landlord can ask the tenant to leave at any time; rents can be increased; rules and expectations can be changed. (Usually some notice is required by law if tenant is asked to move.) The one advantage is that it allows flexibility for the tenant who may choose to move at any time.

LEASE

This rental agreement is in writing. Leases are often on lengthy preprinted forms that are difficult to read because of the legal terminology. A lease includes: names of landlord and tenant; description of the property; length of time of rental; late charges for overdue rent; rules and regulations; security deposit amount; notice requirements for terminating the lease; tenant's rights and responsibilities.

The disadvantage of this type of agreement is that you are legally responsible for the length of the lease even if you are unable to continue living there. The advantages are that there is security in the length of time you can stay, security of no rent increases during the length of the lease term, and a greater understanding of what the landlord expects.

WRITTEN AGREEMENT

This rental agreement is a short form that is less formal than a lease. It often allows month to month rental and lets the landlord write in whatever provision he/she chooses. The renter also has the opportunity to negotiate changes. All changes should be initialed by all parties. The advantages and disadvantages are similar to the written lease. An advantage over the written lease is that it is less complicated and more easily understood.

ORAL AGREEMENT

This rental agreement is talked through by the renter and the landlord. The disadvantage of this agreement is that the renter is not protected since there is little proof of arrangements made.

What Do I Need to Know About Security Deposits?

A security deposit helps the landlord put the rental property back as it was before the renter took over. It can be used only for any damages done, not general maintenance. This deposit protects the landlord and encourages tenants to care for the property and to live up to the conditions of the lease.

The cost of the deposit is usually the amount of one month's rent. Sometimes it's more. Legally it is not normally used to pay for the last month's rent. States set up regulations. You can check in the telephone book for the state's attorney general's office or consumer protection office if you want to know more.

States may require that security deposit money be put into an interest-earning account with the owner receiving only a percentage. (The rest of the interest must be paid annually to the renter.) Or states may require that the tenant be notified in writing of any deductions made from the security deposit. (The rest must be paid back within a limited time frame.)

> **To protect the return of your security deposit, be sure to inspect the premises of your rental unit with your landlord and put in specific writing (usually a checklist) all the problems with the unit!! (This includes marks on walls, spots on carpets, damaged doors, refrigerator nicks, and loose drawer faces.) Then both landlord and renters must sign the checklist.**

If the landlord is reluctant to do this, it is best not to rent the unit. Remember that the person with whom you are making the agreements and commitments may not be the person who owns the premises when you leave the unit. You need everything in writing. This is not just a matter of trust. It is a matter of good business.

What Must I Know Before Signing a Lease?

Signing a lease is a scary step when you are faced with unfamiliar legal terms. It is also scary because you realize that without question, you are now legally responsible on your own. If you don't understand, take it to someone who does. Any fair landlord should allow you to do this. The landlord who says "It's OK to sign it. It's only a standard form lease!" can cause you problems that you may not suspect.

> **Don't sign anything until you understand all of the writing in the document!!!!**

INFORMATION THAT SHOULD BE ON A LEASE

Names

Names on the lease should include the name of the landlord and names of persons who will be living in and responsible for the unit. **(Be absolutely sure that <u>all</u> persons living in the unit have their names on the lease and that there is joint responsibility clearly stated** in case one person moves out! Note what the rental fee is for each person.)

Paying Rent

Rent paying information should include:
- the correct amount of rent and the person to whom you should pay
- the date the rent payments are due
- late charges for overdue rent
- what happens when lease expires
- length of the term of the lease (Leases for a year or longer should be in writing to be effective. Some leases are as brief as three months.)
- if rent can be raised or other lease changes can be

made and, if so, how you will be notified

- if there is a cost-escalator clause that can raise your rent to cover items such as increased taxes or utility costs and improvements.

Moving Out or Subleasing

Moving or subleasing information should include:

- when your notice must be given to the landlord before you move
- if you can sublease the apartment to someone else (Remember that subleasing only means that someone else will pay the cost of the rent, **but you are still responsible for damages and any unpaid rent!**)
- if rent increases when another person is added to the lease
- how many days' notice must be given by the landlord if he/she wants you to move.

Rules and Regulations of the Management

Lease should include information about:

- allowance of pets, children, waterbeds or pianos
- noise restrictions
- decoration and remodeling rules
- use of nails for hanging pictures
- when landlord can enter unit
- who is allowed to live with you
- rules for use of the dwelling (Watch out for "....Tenants will not use the premises for any purpose other than that of a dwelling for the tenants and immediate family.")

Maintenance

Lease should identify responsibilities of maintenance:

- who tends the yard and shovels the snow
- who handles maintenance and repair problems
- whom to contact for problems (name and address, too).

What is Furnished

Lease should state:

- laundry and recreational facilities included
- appliances furnished
- parking facilities and their cost
- who is responsible for utility and heating bills.

Extra Charges

Lease should tell:

- if landlord's liability for accidents in the building is limited to a certain amount
- what deposits and/or payments must be made before you move in
- whether there are any utility connection fees (You may have to check with companies.)
- if the security deposit acts as your last month's rent.

Legal Fees/Disasters

Lease should state:

- what happens if the dwelling is uninhabitable due to a disaster such as fire
- who pays legal fees if there is a dispute between you and the landlord (**Watch out for the statement that you agree "to pay all costs for court proceedings."**)

SPECIAL WARNINGS!

- **No** empty blanks should be left on the lease form.
- Delete, by crossing out on all copies, what you can't live with and agree upon with the landlord.
- If changes are made in lease, you and landlord should initial changes.
- Don't sign a lease on a living space that is not yet completed. You run the risk of paying for a place where you can't live.
- Keep a copy of the agreement in a safe place.
- Read and understand every word and term of the rental agreement or take it to someone who does.
- **Note damages or changes** that you find in the apartment.
- Any damages to the unit or changes to be made by the landlord should be in writing with a completion date. The agreement should be signed by you and the landlord.
- If there are damages to the apartment that haven't been repaired when you move in, they should be clearly stated on the rental agreement or you may end up paying for them when you leave.
- **Negotiate if necessary to get what you need or want to remove in the contract.**

What Can I Do If I Have to Move Before My Lease Expires?

Sometimes unexpected things like illness, job change, or marriage can cause plans to change so that you want to move before the end of your lease. There are things that you can do.

- Pay the rent to the end of the contract (lease) term. You will still be responsible to keep unit safe.
- Contact the landlord and explain your intent to leave and make arrangements to get a new renter. Usually the lease requires the landlord to try to rerent the unit. Until the unit is rented again, you are responsible for the unit. Be sure to contact the landlord as quickly as you can after you learn of your change of plans.
- Sublet the rental unit. Be sure that your lease allows you to sublet but remember that you are still responsible for the rent and any damages incurred.
- Get a sublease in writing with the same terms as on your own lease. (The landlord may be willing to void your lease and create a new one.) If you choose to sublease: check references; get as large a security deposit as possible; check that the monthly payment is made if it is made directly to the landlord, so you aren't stuck with rent and/or damages.

What Can I Do If I Have a Rental Problem?

Before you take any action on a disagreement with your landlord, check out the laws of your state. If the laws do not protect tenants, your disagreement action could get you evicted and cost you legal fees and damages. You can check with the local housing authorities, social service welfare agencies, legal aid services, or clerk of the Landlord-Tenant Court.

#1 You can:

Write to the landlord, politely expressing your problem specifically. Give the landlord a chance to respond favorably. Keep a copy of the letter. It's best to send the letter by registered mail as proof.

#2 If you get no response:

If the repairs or concerns are not cared for in a reasonable time (usually 30 days), do the two following things at the same time.

(1) Complain formally in writing to the government unit of housing authority asking for an inspection. (This process could make a landlord angry since you contacted someone else. Most states can protect you from a retaliatory eviction if you have followed this process.)

(2) Talk directly to the landlord about the problem. If this direct contact is successful, you should call the housing authority to cancel the inspection.

#3 If all efforts have failed:

- Contact an experienced local agency for information. (If your apartment has a tenant's organization, contact them.)
- You may sue in a small claims court, have repairs made and deduct charges from your rent, or refuse to pay the rent. (Refusing to pay the rent may cause eviction unless a lawyer and judge are involved.)
- Housing authorities can be helpful if a building doesn't meet local building codes. Courts have held that landlords can't evict because of reports of violations.

What Are My Responsibilities When Renting?

When you use another person's property, treat it as you would want people to treat it if you owned it. Following this rule will not only help your landlord, but it will also work for your benefit. You can assure a good credit rating and a good reference when you want to move somewhere else. You can protect your security deposit and credit rating. You can create good habits, a good reputation, and good relationships with others who may become your friends. The impressions you make on others often show up in unexpected places, so a good image can be helpful. You can stay safer and healthier.

SUGGESTIONS:

Be a good neighbor:

- Keep the unit clean and safe. (Don't invite mice and bugs in to "bug" your neighbors too.)
- Get rid of all your waste in a clean and safe manner.
- Do not disturb other renters with loud noises, unruly guests, or bad manners.
- Do not use the premises for unlawful purposes.
- If pets are allowed, don't let them disturb neighbors, create offensive odors, or destroy property.
- Send change of address cards to people who sent mail to you.

Be a good tenant:

- Do not destroy or damage any part of the unit.
- Understand and follow all the regulations set up in your lease.
- Use all appliances, plumbing, and electrical and heating facilities in a safe way. Keep them and the unit as clean as conditions permit.
- Pay your rent and utilities promptly when due.
- Inform your landlord in a written, legal way that you plan to move.
- Report all problems to the landlord, including ones you may have caused.

Staying Safe

"How can I stay safe in today's world?"

New surroundings offer new challenges. Staying SAFE is a challenge in itself since everyone is a probable crime or accident victim. Prepare by recognizing possible problems and thinking through possibilities before they happen.

Equipment and Buildings May Be Different Where You Move. You may have come from a home that had many of the latest conveniences and discover that what you can find and/or can afford isn't what you're used to. An apartment may have different types of entrances and locations. You may end up with a space heater rather than central heating...old floor lamps from Grandma's attic that have brittle cords rather than ceiling lights or new lamps...a gas stove rather than an electric one.

Community and Values May Differ Where You Move. You may also have felt safe enough at home to leave the doors unlocked...trust a newfound friend... leave packages in your unlocked car while you shopped...walk safely to or from your car. You may not be in such a safe environment when you are on your own.

Beat Burglars and Intruders!

- Display "BEWARE" signs. If you have a dog or an alarm system, the sign may deter burglars. Some alarm system signs advertising the maker can also give information to help burglars disarm the system. Research systems in consumer magazines.
- Do not leave keys under a flower pot, on a window ledge, or under a mat. Burglars look there first.
- You can leave a key with a trusted neighbor or friend for emergencies.
- If you misplace your keys, replace your locks.
- Don't leave tools and ladders where a thief can use them for entry.
- Be sure your landlord changes your locks for you before you move in.
- Participate in a neighborhood watch if you can.

- Motion detectors can be effective deterrents.
- If you leave your car at an airport, remove any identification that would aid a thief.

MAKE YOUR HOME LOOK OCCUPIED

- Leave your radio on.
- Turn down the telephone bell volume so an unanswered telephone isn't heard.
- Keep garage door down. Keep garage doors locked or disconnected. Keep windows covered.
- Leave interior lights on, especially in inside rooms of the house. Use timers on lights, radios, or TVs.
- Leave some shades open, or in their normal position.
- NEVER leave a note attached to your door.

IF YOU LEAVE FOR A PERIOD OF TIME

- Have neighbors use your garbage cans. Spotters for burglary rings may work for refuse collectors.
- Have your neighbor pick up mail, newspapers, and circulars.
- Have your driveway and walks cleared of snow.
- Don't inform any people carelessly of your absence. You can be overheard.
- Ask neighbors to use your driveway sometimes while you are gone.

KEEP WINDOWS SAFE

- Protect windows that are accessible from the ground level or reachable level (over porch, garage, outside staircases, fire escapes, or even another building with a board placed between two areas.) Prepare them so they can't be opened enough to allow entry.

- Stop entry through a double hung window (two panels, one or both of which slide up and down) by drilling a hole into the window tracks on both sides of the window. Place the holes so window can't be opened when a nail or bolt is placed in the hole. Keep heads visible so they can be easily removed in case of fire.

- Holes can also be drilled through the bottom sash and halfway into the upper sash to keep the window from opening far enough for entry but allowing air circulation. Place a ten penny nail or bolt in holes to keep window from opening too far. Nail or bolt head should be visible for easy removal.

- Leave windows alone that are painted shut in older houses unless there aren't other fire exits.

- Use long enough screws to secure a window air conditioner to both window and the frame so it can't be easily removed for entry.

- Cover all windows with shades or curtains.

- Don't leave any desirable items where they can be easily seen (i.e. purse, wallet, electronics).

Protect your windows too!

Buy Locks

- There are key-operated window locks available in hardware stores and locksmiths.

- Casement windows which are operated with cranks are usually more secure because they don't allow enough space for human entry. There are locks available for these.

Check Putty and Crawl Spaces

- Check the putty that holds window panes in their frames (especially in older houses) to make sure that the panes are not easily removed.

- Check any crawl space entry that could be used such as attics, crawl spaces, and coal chutes!

KEEP DOORS SAFE

Doors can become the easiest entry for intruders. Metal or solid core doors of oak are the safest. These may not always be available where you live. You can, however, cut the potential of entry by others.

Always Lock Your Doors and Windows!

Use Locks and Bolts

- If you have double hung doors (two doors placed side by side), flush lever bolts need to be installed in the edge of the door at the top and at the bottom so they can't be jimmied open. (Buy at hardware store.)

- Deadbolt locks are the safest. Be sure that the bolt extends at least one inch beyond the door edge. Standard door locks can be opened by using credit cards, wires, and screw drivers!

- Door chains can be useful but should be put on so that a hand can't reach inside to release them. A chain opened with a key is best.

Check Hinges and Fit

- Be sure that door hinges are placed on the <u>inside</u> of your house especially at garage entrance so hinges can't be removed for easy entry. If hinges are on the outside, weld or flange with a hammer for harder removal. Insert a setscrew or flatheaded screw through a portion of the hinge that is not exposed when door is closed.

- The door should fit well so that it is difficult to force open. You can add weather stripping to fill the space between the frame and the door if needed.

Take Extra Precautions

- Peepholes can be helpful in distinguishing who is at the door before you open it.
- Windows at the outside doors are easily opened with the help of a glass cutter.

Patio Door Precautions

- Doors should fit well on the frame to avoid lifting or tilting. Check problems with landlord.
- Cut a broom handle to fit the door channel at floor level. It can be removed to open from the inside.
- If there are not adjustments at top or bottom of doors to create tight fits, secure two or three screws in the overhead track to reduce chance of entry. Make sure screws allow doors to slide.

TELEPHONE SAFETY

- Beware of telephone surveys. Don't give information that can be used by burglars. (i.e. "Do you have a dog?" "Do you live alone?" "What is your age?" "Do you own a computer?" "Do you work?")
- Strangers can find out when you are home with a simple question, "When may I call?"
- Use only your initials in the telephone book so a caller won't know your sex.
- If you are harassed by phone, call your telephone company and the police.
- Beware of people seeking information about you or others whom you know. Even be concerned about identification as a police person. Make the excuse that you can't talk. Check the phone number. Call back after verifying the person has legitimate reason for questioning. If the number is false, call police.
- Never leave information on an answering device explaining when you can be contacted.
- You can use a male voice on an answering machine. (Background voices imply that others live there.)

Cordless or cellular phones

- Eavesdropping is a hobby. People use scanners to pick up thousands of frequencies and use them to listen. Never discuss confidential personal or business matters when using cordless or cellular phones.

KEEP BASEMENTS SAFE

- Make sure laundry and storage areas are secure. Check outside entries including basement windows.
- If you are unacquainted with your neighbors, use a buddy system when going into a laundry area.
- Use basement when people are awake in the building. (2 A.M. laundry time is not good!)

KEEP PARKING AREA SAFE

- Make sure that the area for parking and the walkway to doors are well lit.
- Bushes should be low so that there are no hiding places, especially at night.
- Park quickly. Look around before stopping car and unlocking door.
- Do not have your name on a reserved stall to signify that you are not at home.

Check under car as you approach!

Entering or Leaving

- Have apartment (house) key in your hand, not in pocket or purse when leaving the car.
- Don't carry full armloads if possible. Doors will be hard to open.
- Keep your car locked at all times.
- Be sure to check the back seat of the car for uninvited guests before you enter.
- Walk tall. Look as if you are able to protect yourself!

Other Safety Hints

- Don't put your name on your car license. It invites trouble!
- If a person follows your car, drive directly to a police station. If the follower is still behind you, honk your horn until someone comes out of the station.
- If you are a woman, you might consider wearing a man's hat at night while you drive.
- Consider carrying a whistle with you to use if you need help.
- Never leave your house key on your ignition key ring. Duplicates of the house key can be quickly made when you give your keys to a valet or parking lot attendant!
- Codes of electronic car door openers can be picked up. Cars can then be stolen or persons can let themselves in while you're gone.

KEEP ENTRY AREA SAFE

- Be sure the door closes behind you when you enter.
- Do not allow anyone whom you do not know to enter when you open the door.
- If you pick up your mail at the entrance, wait until you get inside before you read it.
- Be sure all entrances, including basement and back doors, are secure.
- Do not use your first name on your mailbox. Use only initials.
- If elevators are used, do not enter an elevator with anyone who is suspicious looking.
- Stairways have hidden corners that make good hiding places.
- Never allow strangers or solicitors into your house. Get a person's credentials and then check them by phone. People entering your house may be sizing it up for the future. Get GOOD identification.
- If someone tries to grab you, yell "Police," "Thief," or "Fire" to attract attention.
- Stay alert!

INSURE AGAINST ROBBERY, FIRE, AND ACCIDENTS

- Buy renter's insurance. You may want to prepare for the worst and have enough home owner's insurance to pay for any loss. A special "rider" is needed for valuables. Talk to an insurance agent.
- Keep a permanent record of all that you own for insurance purposes in case of fire or burglary. Video tapes are good records. Explain information about articles as you tape.
- Special jewelry should be in a bank safety deposit box. If you must keep it at home, store in a safe that is really safe. You can hide things in baseboards, switch plates, and ceilings.
- Mark your belongings with an electric engraver. Police may loan engravers.
- If you leave your car at an airport, remove any identification that would aid a thief.
- If you come home and suspect you have been robbed, **do NOT enter the house!** Call police to enter with you. Don't disturb anything that could be used for evidence.

PROTECT YOUR ATM CARD

Automatic teller machine cards such as TYME and Mastercard need to be protected too.

- Don't let "con artists" convince you to draw money from your account. Report them to the police.
- Look around for any suspicious people or circumstances as you approach your ATM machine. Leave immediately if you are suspicious.
- Have your ATM card ready before you approach the machine and move away quickly.
- Do NOT count your money or even expose how much you have until you are away from the machine.
- Do keep your transaction receipt to check against your bank statement.
- Never give your PIN number to anyone.
- Make sure that no one sees you punch in your PIN number. Position your body so no one can look.

- If you lose your card or have questions about your billing, call the company which is on the card.
- In case of theft, contact the company and police immediately.

PROTECT YOUR SOCIAL SECURITY NUMBER

A stolen social security number can be used to apply for a credit card. Unpaid charges can be run up to destroy your credit rating. To keep your number safe:

- Don't carry your social security card in your billfold or purse. Keep it in a secure place at home.
- If an employer requests your social security number for identification, ask that the numbers be moved. Digits can be moved around or middle numbers can be replaced with zeros.
- Never give your number to a business unless absolutely necessary.
- Don't enter contests that require your number.
- File a request for a "personalized earnings and benefits estimate" from Social Security records about every three years to check for any unusual entries.

Protect Yourself From Fire!!!

Use Smoke Detectors

- Have smoke detectors in strategic spots (i.e. near every bedroom and at top of all major stairways).
- Check batteries in smoke detectors regularly. There is usually a button visible for testing.

Be Careful of Cigarettes and Flammables

- Never smoke in bed or a chair where you may fall asleep. Put burned cigarettes in safe containers.
- Keep flammables such as paint and turpentine away from furnace area.
- NEVER squirt lighter fluid from a can onto a fire or hot coals. The can may explode in your hand. (Flame travels back on the fluid.)
- Don't keep oily or paint rags. Dispose of them so they do not cause spontaneous combustion.

Use Space Heaters Wisely

- Place any space heater away from places where people walk.
- Keep curtains, blankets, clothes, and rugs away from baseboard and free standing gas or electric heaters.
- Check gas heaters to see they are in good working order. Dangerous carbon monoxide doesn't smell.

Use Appliances Safely

- If you smell gas, don't turn on a stove, heater, or light. Call the gas company to check for a gas leak. Service usually comes quickly. The smell can indicate a pilot light that's not lit or a dangerous leak.
- Allow air to circulate around appliances such as televisions, radios, stereos, and microwave ovens.

General Safety Precautions to Practice

- Do not put clothes or cloth over lamps. Light bulbs are hot enough to start a fire.
- Avoid clutter especially around a furnace or on stairways that will block your exit.
- Check to see that windows are easily opened to allow you to escape from a fire.
- If you have a fireplace, use a fireplace screen.
- Keep the number of the fire department close to the telephone.
- If your clothes catch on fire, **stop!** Drop to the ground, then roll back and forth to smother flames. Running fans flames.
- Develop the habit of sleeping with your door closed.
- Keep a flashlight close to your bed in case there's no electricity to use.

Practice Escape Before Fire Occurs

- Have a fire ladder available on upper stories of a house where there are no outlets onto a garage, porch, or fire escape. Fire ladders are available in hardware stores. Ask fire department for advice.
- Know how to use the ladder and try it! Practice a fire drill to prepare for an emergency.
- Plan two escape routes. If you are living with someone, plan somewhere that you can meet so

that you don't try to save the person if he/she is already safe.

Check Electrical Uses

- If any electrical system is not working properly, check it immediately!
- Do not overload a circuit. Use only **one** high wattage appliance at a time in a single outlet. (High wattage appliances include: toaster ovens, microwaves, refrigerators, waffle irons, coffee pots, hair dryers, toasters, irons.)
- Don't use triple plugs or extension cords. Use heavy duty cords on appliances that produce heat.
- Don't place cords under rugs.
- Don't leave appliance cords attached to outlets after disconnecting the cord from the appliance especially around a sink area where water may get into the connection.
- Don't make wires bare by jerking them from outlets, winding them tightly around appliances, or placing them over hoods, through doors, or partition openings.
- Replace frayed, cracked cords.
- If wall outlets or switches are warm to the touch, check them. Warmth indicates unsafe wiring!
- Don't replace fuses with pennies or wire. Use only new fuses (15AMP is correct for most circuits).
- All appliances should have Underwriter's Laboratory (UL) or Canadian Standard Association (CSA) seals of safety on them.

Avoid Kitchen Fires

- Have fire extinguisher available in the kitchen where you can quickly reach it. Know how to use it.
- Do NOT throw water on a grease fire. Use baking soda or a fire extinguisher rated general purpose.
- Have a smoke detector in the kitchen area.
- Stop a fire in a pan by holding lid on tightly to keep oxygen out.
- Keep paper towels, cloth towels, pot holders, and plastics away from range burners.
- Don't remove hot pans from oven with wet, or even damp, dish towels. Steam creates burns.

- Don't use a dish towel to remove a pan from the range burner or oven. Towels drag and catch fire.
- Watch out for loose clothing or hair that can catch fire over a burner.

Make an Escape Plan in Case of Fire and Practice!

- If there are others in your apartment, make a plan of where to meet in case of fire.
- Don't panic.
- When you smell smoke, alert everyone you can and get out quickly!
- Do not return to the building!
- Breathing smoke is dangerous. Running and breathing deeply can kill you because of poisonous gases produced. Cover your mouth and move quickly close to the floor.

PLAN #1

If Door Is Closed and the Handle Is Hot!

- If you are in bed when you smell smoke, roll out. Crawl, keeping your head close to the floor. If you can, cover your mouth with a wet cloth, breathe through it with short breaths.
- Check to see if the door handle is hot. If it is, exit through a window if you can.
- If windows can't be opened, break the window or screen. Protect yourself from broken glass.
- Use a fire ladder if one is available and if you can't, climb onto a porch or garage.
- If you must jump, hang from the window sill so you fall from less height.
- If you can't get out, go to plan #3.

PLAN #2

If Door Is Shut, Handle Isn't Hot and Pressure Hasn't Built Against Door

- Grab something such as a pillow to cover your nose and mouth to protect from smoke.
- Stay low, very close to the floor.
- Feel the door handle for warmth. If cool, open door slowly. Brace yourself in case fire pressure has built up outside the door. If there is pressure, close door and go back to Plan #1.
- If there is no pressure, use stairways instead of elevators. Elevators may lack power.
- Move fast! Fire moves unbelievably quickly!

PLAN #3

If You Are Trapped!!!

- Close the door and seal it as well as you can. Use sheets, clothes, or towels. If water is handy, wet them. They will give more protection.
- Keep your head close to the floor where there is less smoke and more oxygen.
- Open a window only wide enough to signal that you need help. You could wave a sheet or a piece of clothing. Breathe the fresh air from the window. Then wait for rescue.

PLAN #4

If You are In a Large Hotel or Apartment Building

- **Preplan when you arrive.** Find nearest fire exit. Count doors from your door to the exit and see that the exit door opens. Then check to see how windows open. Read fire instruction posted on your door.
- If you smell smoke or know there is a fire in the building, grab a pillow or wet towel to breathe through. Stay close to the floor and take short breaths. Check doorknob for heat before going into hall.
- Even if doorknob is cool, brace yourself for pressure build-up outside before opening a door.
- Do not stop to take anything with you **but your key.** Fire spreads fast!
- Your key will allow you to reenter your room if fire blocks your exit.
- If you must return to your room, block all door openings and air inlets with wet towels and clothes.
- Throw water on the walls and door.
- Open the window only far enough to signal for help and breathe fresh air.

INTERNET SAFETY
Personal Safety Online

Give personal information only to those you trust. It may feel safe, but it may not be. Be wary of giving information such as age, marital status or financial information. Don't give identifying information such as phone number, home address, or school name in chat rooms or bulletin boards.

- Never send a person a picture of yourself.
- Your E-mail address will be available to others from placing your name in a member directory to a bulletin board, automated mailing list or newsgroup, or by participating in a chat session.
- Never respond to messages on bulletin boards that are suggestive, obscene, belligerent, threatening, or make you feel uncomfortable.
- Be careful if someone offers you something for nothing such as gifts and money.
- Be careful of offers that involve your coming to a meeting or having someone visit your house. Face to face meetings can be dangerous.

Special Warnings

- Verify through a third party whom you know and trust, the identity of a person met on the internet. Find ways to check any information.
- If you choose to meet with a person: take a friend along; meet in a public, well lit place; stay near other people. Set conditions for meeting and stick to them. Provide your own transportation to and from the meeting.

Online Ordering

- Don't deal with companies that have only a PO box number and no telephone.
- Do business only with reputable vendors.
- Never transmit credit card numbers, financial institution data, or personal identifiable account numbers unless confident of the business.
- You have some security only when the virtual store has set up a secure connection.
- A business only needs your name, credit card account number, and expiration date.
- Be sure to know the refund policy.
- When ordering, print a copy, save it. Note URL of site and confirmation number. If you use a credit card number rather than a check, you can challenge a charge. Check statements for unauthorized transactions. If there is an error, contact the credit card company

Other Things to Consider

- Avoid unwanted solicitations and surveys.
- Change password frequently. Don't give password to anyone online. The safest password uses six or more characters with mixed letters or numbers.

Finding a Compatible Roommate

"How can I find a roommate that's right for me?"

Friend or Foe?

Renting often involves finding a roommate. If you choose the right one, you can gain a friend and save money. If you choose the wrong one, you can gain trouble. Imagine:

- A roommate who has to have music playing all night long for a "security blanket."
- A "neat" living with a "slob" who leaves a trail of clothes, cans, cigarette butts, and dirty dishes.
- Arriving home to find police making a drug raid on your roommate's bedroom.
- A roommate moving in the middle of a lease term, leaving unpaid rent and telephone bills.

Step #1 Find a Compatible Roommate

There are guidelines for finding a compatible roommate from among friends, strangers, or one assigned to you. A good beginning is to communicate. You might consider using a compatibility checklist with potential roommates to discover each other's tolerance levels. The list can give you an opportunity to talk before you share your space. Compromises can be reached ahead of time so disagreements may be avoided. This may sound formal, but it could be fun! Each person should complete the list, then talk together about your responses.

COMPATIBILITY CHART

	OK	Tolerable	No Way!
Personality:			
Lazy			
Outgoing, laughs easily			
Short tempered			
Oversensitive			
Self centered			
Dishonest			
Is a prude			
Quiet			
Always late			
TV "couch potato"			
Sleeping Habits:			
Snores			

	OK	Tolerable	No Way!
Stays up late at night			
Early riser			
Sleep walks			
Reads before sleeping			
Sleeps with window open			
Needs music to go to sleep			
Eating Habits:			
Grazes, snacks a lot			
Prefers to cook at home			
Eats out often			
Uses pre-prepared food			
"Picky" eater			
Has bad nutritional habits			
Buys expensive food			
Has many guests to feed			
Personal Habits			
No respect for privacy			
Doesn't budget			
Does drugs			
Drinks alcohol often			
Borrows money			
Smokes			
Talks a lot			
Procrastinates			
"Hogs" the phone			
Has annoying hobby			
Housekeeping Attitudes:			
Clutters			
Overly neat and clean			
Wants a pet			
Lets dirty dishes stack up			
Doesn't like or share housework			
Believes that "messy" is comfortable			
Hangs wet laundry in bathroom			
Social Habits:			
"Parties" often			
Invites friend of opposite sex overnight			
Likes overnight guests of same sex			
Stays home most of the time			
Likes to entertain, goes out nights			
Hates sports			
Likes classical or rock music			
Religious			

It's important to know as much as you can about a potential roommate.

OFF TO AN APARTMENT WITH A FRIEND?

When you have someone that you know to share your living space, you have some advantage compared to starting out with a stranger. Best friends, however, can end up "enemies" after living together for a while. Some problems can be avoided by talking together and preplanning before living together. Try the *Compatibility Chart.* Expectations can be very different for each of you!

If you consider living with someone of the opposite sex, there are additional questions to consider. Communication becomes even more important. If your body goes along with the living space, great risk is involved. In addition to questions in the *Compatibility Chart,* consider and talk together about:

- religion
- family values
- affect on personal future aspirations
- pregnancy
- venereal diseases
- emotional impact on your future
- infidelity
- male/female roles
- community values
- role of friends
- birth control
- "break-up" possibility and plans

Finding a roommate among strangers?

When you must find a roommate from people you don't know, do a background check. Finding out as much information as you can about a potential roommate is not an invasion of privacy. **You will be creating a business contract that involves your money, your time, and your life!**

In today's world, safety has become increasingly important. You can rely on a reputable rental agency if you don't know people. Double check with any friend, co-worker, or acquaintance of the potential roommate by asking questions. Be concerned if anyone reports that the person has a violent temper, mistreats animals, uses drugs, drinks in excess, is dishonest, or has angry outbursts. **(Be sure to check with persons other than those used as references. Friends may cover up damaging information.)**

- If you question a person's criminal background, get social security and driver's license numbers. Check with the district attorney's office, the sheriff, or the police department for information. Also check the driving record and court records for bankruptcy filings or criminal activity.
- Interview person carefully. Ask for references, place of employment and banking, date of birth, last two addresses. Verify place of employment and check any references, especially the previous landlord.

> **People should be willing to give this information and will probably want the same from you. You want to feel safe with the person in the room next to yours!!!**

OFF TO A COLLEGE DORM ROOM?

College roommates are usually predetermined for you when you first enter. Some schools do minimal "matching" of students for their ages and lifestyles. Notification may be sent to you. This is one time you will have to learn to get along with the person assigned to you. However, if persons are totally incompatible, there are provisions made for change.

There are many advantages to dorm room living as you are starting out into a new life. People have similar interests. Many things such as activities, food, safety, and rules can be taken care of for you. Disadvantages include lack of privacy, different schedules, limited space, and noise.

If you do choose a dormitory or residence hall on campus, it is a good idea to contact your new roommate, as soon as you find out who it will be, so that you can become acquainted and also compare notes of what each of you will bring to your room.

You can set up each person's responsibilities and get to know each other. A contract can be helpful. (See *Compatibility Guide* and the following *Informal Roommate Contract*.) Questions should cover:

Overnight guests   Shared equipment
Study hours   Snack patterns
Borrowing   Shared expenses
Sleeping patterns   Use of space
Cleaning

WHERE WERE YOU?!?

STEP #2 Protect Yourself... Create a Business Contract

Incompatible personalities or lifestyles can cause real misery. At home, rules are set so you know what is tolerated and expected. When starting a relationship of living together rules are important too. You are not only sharing living space, you are also extending credit in some form. A business contract that includes use of space and shared resources is helpful. Interview each other at length. Clarify information about:
- Use of the rooms.
- Schedule for use of bathroom if there is only one.

- "Off limits" of your own bedroom.
- Advance notice required for invitations to boyfriends and girlfriends.
- Distribution of keys.
- Telephone usage including taking of messages if you have no answering machine.
- Payment of bills.

CREATING A BUSINESS CONTRACT

The following contract is an example of an informal way to reach agreement on sharing your living space. If you prefer a legal agreement, you should contact a lawyer.

**When you fill out the contract,
you should check it against your lease.**

INFORMAL ROOMMATE CONTRACT

FINANCES

Address of unit to be rented _____

Date agreement begins _____

                              (Month)   (Date)   (Year)

I.   **Roommates renting unit:**

    Roommate #1 _____

      Present Address _____

    Roommate #2 _____

      Present Address _____

    Roommate #3 _____

      Present Address _____

II.   **Rent: (Check appropriate statement and complete or mark out blank lines)**

    Rent amount for the unit is _____ per_____

    Date when rent payment is due _____

    This rent payment includes the following utilities: _____

    _____

    _____

III.   **Utilities: (Check appropriate statement and complete or mark out blank lines)**

    Utilities not covered by rent:

    ❏ Gas bill will be paid by (name) _____

      Names on billing will include: _____

    ❏ Electricity bill will be paid by (name) _____

      Names on billing will include: _____

    ❏ Water/sewer bill will be paid by (name) _____

      Names on billing will include: _____

    ❏ Other utility bills (explain): _____

      Will be paid by (name) _____

      Names on billing will include: _____

    ❏ **All persons will share equally in the payment of rent and utilities.**

IV.   **Telephone: (Check appropriate statement and complete or mark out blank lines)**

    ❏ Telephone bill will be paid by (name)_____

      Names on billing will include: _____

    _____

    ❏ Each roommate will pay equal portion of base bill.

    ❏ Each roommate will pay his/her personal long distance calls.

V.   **Security deposit:**

_____ will pay_____

_____ will pay_____

_____ will pay_____

The amounts will be paid back when security deposit is returned when he/she moves out.

VI. **Moving out:**

When a roommate moves, _____days notice will be given. If proper notice isn't given, the roommate must pay his/her share of rent until the notice period is up.

When moving out: (Check appropriate spaces)

_____ All roommates agree to move out at same time on: Date_____

_____ If, for any reason, a roommate must move, he/she will continue to pay his/her share of rent and bills to end of lease.

_____ If, for any reason, a roommate moves before lease ends, he/she may replace self with a substitute roommate that is agreed upon by remaining roommates. No financial loss should be left for the remaining roommates.

_____ If any damage is done to the unit, whoever caused the damage must pay for it.

_____ Cleaning up process will be shared before anyone moves.

_____ If there are costs that will be charged from the security deposit, each roommate will pay his/her share.

_____ Other:_____
_____

VII. **Food:**

_____ Each roommate will buy his/her own food.

_____ Groceries will be purchased and shared equally.

_____ Personal food will be "borrowed" only with permission and will be paid for or replaced as agreed.

_____Other: _____
_____

VIII. **Shared equipment and furnishings:**

The shared furnishings will be handled as follows when roommates move out:

Equipment	Original cost	Who will pay share & keep	Who will sell & split proceeds

Damage done to shared furnishings should be repaired or paid for by mutual agreement.

IX. **Renter's insurance:**

(This insurance should be carefully checked with your insurance agent!)

_____Renter's insurance will be paid for by (name)_____

The insurance will be paid directly to _____
_____

Other plan: _____
_____

SPACE SHARING AGREEMENTS

Laundry:

Each roommate will do his/her personal laundry at_____

Shared laundry will be handled in the following manner:_____

JOB SHARING AGREEMENTS

Job	When to be done (week, day, etc.)	Done by

Quiet hours for radio, TV, stereo, etc. are:_____Weekdays _____Weekends

Guests: Overnight guest limits_____ Number_____ How often_____

Other guest limits_____ Number_____ How often_____

Hobby Limits:

Hobbies_____

Limits _____

Building a Support Network

"How can I find new friends and get help when I need it?"

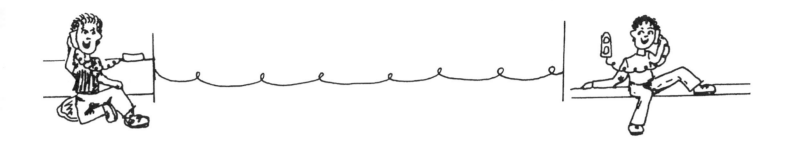

When you take off on your own, it will be helpful to build a greater support network of people **nearby** to fill in for what family, friends, and professionals have provided for you in the past. This network included people you know such as friends, relatives, friends of relatives and friends, teachers, employers, people with whom you worked, organization members, neighbors, your doctor, and other professionals. They helped you by sharing information, contacts, assistance, and thoughts.

If you continue to stay in the town where you live, you can benefit from a growing network. If you are going on a campus, you'll find a ready-made network of support people including people your age who need friends and support too. If you are leaving your town, you will need to develop this additional network and it will be more difficult, but the advantage is that you have a chance to start fresh. The support groups you choose, the friends you make…even the professionals you choose to help you, can affect your future. You, in return, affect theirs.

Types of Networking

Networking is a technique that you use throughout your life. It involves benefits for everyone. The people and organizations in your network offer support when you need it. They prevent loneliness, give advice, share fun, help find jobs, direct your spirituality, offer emotional support, help you stay healthy, and share their resources. There are informal and formal networks.

Informal Networks

FRIENDS

Life can be lonely without friends, especially when you have moved into strange surroundings. Loneliness is a normal part of life and is natural when you move into new territory. There is a difference between being alone and being lonely however. Loneliness can be a challenge to grow. If you are lonely…do something! You can make new friends along the way. While you are alone and are creating an additional support network, you should appreciate yourself. **Be your own friend! Enjoy doing what you like to do. Spend time organizing and planning.**

If you are in a school setting, there are many activities in addition to classes. You can choose from the things you like and then start participating in the activities. Ask questions of other students, look at the school paper, and watch bulletin boards and posters. If you are not in a school setting, there are other ways you can become acquainted and make new friends. You must look harder and plan more creatively to make new contacts. If the activities and friends you choose will fit into your future goals, you will have a double advantage.

Make A Plan to Make New Contacts and Avoid Loneliness

1. List what you like to do and what you would like to learn to do. After you review the things that you would really like to do, you can begin to find others to do them with you.

2. Explore Your Community You can act the part of a tourist. Take walking or driving tours by car or bus. Visit churches, libraries, and public meetings. Call about interesting meetings. Read ads and newspapers. Call the Chamber of Commerce for list of organizations. Take time to talk with people around you.

3. Meet New Friends By working together with others in an activity, bonding occurs and friends are made. Just decide what you want to do and then go after it! There are many places to meet new people:

- In community organizations with volunteers in your interest area.
- At free events. You will be surprised with the number of things available from hiking to concerts.
- With sports groups or health clubs. (These interests are replacing the "bar scene.")
- In churches where a wide variety of activities can be found, in addition to religious experiences. (They're good places to create friends of different ages. Often older adults become valuable mentors. Churches can become an extended family. Groups with spiritual orientation offer a feeling of mutual support.)

FAMILY

When you leave home, you still have a family…whatever that form may be. This part of your network stays with you for the rest of your life. It can be wise to keep the relationships healthy. Many young adults become a part of the "Yo-Yo Youth" who have tested their wings and find it necessary to have some further family support along the way. They return home for short periods before starting out again away from home. It's wise to keep a life-line secure. It may need to spring back!

Suggestions for building adult relationships with families:

1. Become a considerate guest, not a child.
2. Review attitudes from different viewpoints other than personal.
3. Leave "baggage" at the doorstep…the "past" is behind. Start where you are today.

4. Treat family members as favorite friends, considering their needs as well as your own.
5. Plan a family "meeting" to avoid problems by setting house rules before you return. Consider:
   - Financial support
   - Noise control
   - Your future plans for making a living
   - Household help
   - Guests of yours
   - Hours that meet needs of all
6. Practice the golden rule of doing unto others as you would have them do to you.
7. Use positive communication techniques such as using "**I**" messages rather than "**You**" messages. (i.e. "**I** would like it if you…" or "**I** feel bad when you…," rather than "**You** always…!," "**You** don't understand!," "**You** should not…")

MEDICAL DOCTORS

When you are sick, you may not have the time or energy to research and find a new doctor. Preplan:

- Choose a doctor before you need one. Many doctors do not take new patients.
- Get a recommendation from your family doctor if you go to a new community. You can also get recommendations from friends, relatives, co-workers, local medical societies, the local hospital, and nurse acquaintances. If you look in the *Yellow Pages*, you will probably find a medical society listed under *Organizations* that can furnish information on doctors in the community.
- Check on the training of your chosen doctor in the library in *Directory of Medical Specialists*. It is wise to get a good recommendation or personally check records.
- Call several doctors before you make your final choice. Ask the following questions:

- If I choose this doctor, are new patients being taken?
- What are the office hours?
- How do I reach the doctor if he/she isn't in the office? Who is the alternative doctor?
- Does the doctor make emergency house calls or do phone consultations on minor problems?
- Is it difficult to get an appointment if a problem is urgent?
- What are charges for routine office visits, revisits, phone consultations, and physicals?
- How and when must payment be made?
- Is a pre-visit necessary before I really need doctor care?
- Is my present insurance acceptable and how are insurance claims made?

> **New laws on health care
> need to be checked regularly.**

- If you can afford it, make an appointment and visit the doctor of your choice to see if you are comfortable and can communicate. Give background information that can be helpful. Carry records with you of blood type, past illnesses, allergies, surgery records, drug sensitivities, vaccinations, shots, and X-rays. (Further information from your previous doctor should be transferred as soon as you choose a new doctor so it is there when you need it. Just write or call for your records to be sent.)

> **HAVE QUICKLY AVAILABLE**
> •Telephone numbers of doctors,
> pharmacists, emergency services.
> •Medical insurance numbers.
> •Medical care book, first aid book,
> and emergency kit.
> •Medical alert bracelet for personal problems
> such as diabetes, allergies.

DENTISTS

Finding a dentist is similar to finding a medical doctor. Preplan before you get a toothache!

- Get a recommendation through your present dentist. Also ask friends, relatives, or coworkers.
- Call the doctor's office to see if new patients are being accepted. If they are, ask questions:
  - How difficult is it to get an appointment?
  - Can arrangements be made easily in case of emergency?
  - Is it necessary to have a pre-visit?
  - What is the charge for teeth cleaning, fillings, pre-visit, and regular visits?
  - How and when is payment made?
  - Is general anesthesia administered in the office? (This is usually done at a hospital.)
- Have your previous records forwarded as directed by the new dentist you have chosen.

> **Regular dental care can save money
> in the long run. In the meantime,
> avoid sweets, brush, and floss!**

WALK-IN CLINICS

In many cities today there are walk-in clinics listed in the *Yellow Pages* that help with emergency care or regular care quickly without an appointment. These clinics are helpful to those who haven't found a family doctor. They are open for long, extended hours for your convenience. This type of clinic can get the help of other doctors if needed. Referral service to specialists is given if appropriate.

COLLEGE HEALTH SERVICES

Medical services vary at each school. Only students can participate in these services. The cost is usually minimal and is often included in tuition charges. It is meaningful to compare the costs of these services with any medical insurance that is available already through your family, work, or a personal policy already in force. Be sure to check. As an example, an unplanned pregnancy can be especially difficult to cover.

PHARMACISTS

One of the best sources of free "health help" is local pharmacists. They are trusted professionals who are trained and licensed. They know the pharmacological aspects of prescribed drugs. They can advise about over-the-counter drugs that are available to relieve symptoms or inform about prescription drugs prescribed by doctors. Information about any allergies, drug reactions, medical conditions, or any other medications being taken should be given to the pharmacist. The pharmacist can quickly check and advise your doctor for you of any possible problems. Computer programs bring instant information about use, reactions, and side effects of medications. This information is very important in helping you to avoid potentially serious problems.

Ask questions when you buy a prescription. (You may receive information on the container or on a special paper. If you have further questions, you can call back and talk to the pharmacist.)

- Is a less expensive generic drug available as a substitute?
- What is the real name of the drug?
- What does the drug do and what are possible side effects?
- Should the medication be taken with or without food?
- How many times a day should the medication be taken and in what amount?
- How long should it be taken?
- How long will it take to relieve symptoms so I can judge if medication is working?
- Are there any limitations while on the medication such as not driving, doing dangerous work, drinking alcohol, or interaction with other drugs being taken?
- How many times can the prescription be refilled?

LEGAL SERVICES

Lawyers

A lawyer may be needed for an issue that takes you to court; requires filing of legal papers; involves a lot of money, time, or property. The type of problem should help make the choice of the lawyer. There are many types of lawyers. Some handle real estate, wills, divorces, small lawsuits, review legal papers such as leases to name a few. To find a lawyer, recommendations can come from persons you respect: friends, relatives, employers, ministers, bankers, law school teachers, administrators, and consumer groups. You can also look in the *Yellow Pages* under LRS (Lawyer Referral Service), call the local, city, county, or state bar associations, or research at the library.

If you have a legal problem, choose two or three lawyers to interview before making a decision. Generally, good lawyers should not ask for fees until their services are actually used. If the lawyer you choose is too busy, he/she can recommend someone else. Call first and ask if the lawyer of your choice will meet with you to discuss your problem. Ask if there is a charge for the first contact. After you explain your problem ask questions.

- Is there a more simple way to handle my problem that would cost less?
- What specialty areas do you normally handle? (It may be wise to make a choice combining areas of expertise such as negotiator, litigator, tax specialist, marital counselor, real estate specialist.)
- Can you give references of similar cases to mine that you've handled?
- How many cases have you won?
- What are the usual results and costs of such cases?
- What are your charges? Are there flat fees charged for specific services? Can charges be limited?
- Are there additional or separate charges in the billing?
- What percentage of time do you normally spend on a case like this one?
- Do you do all basic work or are associates and/or paralegals used?
- How do you keep me informed of the progress of the case?
- What can I expect for a time-line for completion of the case and cost?
- What is the process of payment?
- Can you work a contingency fee* arrangement if I can't afford your regular fees?
- Are you willing to put our agreement in writing?

*A contingency fee allows the lawyer to collect a percentage of the court award. If you receive nothing, so does the lawyer. Usual fees are about 33% of the settlement. You must normally pay court fees and your own expenses.

It is best to put any agreement in writing to avoid misunderstandings and offer protection. Agree upon:

- Estimate of original fee agreement (include: telephone calls, filing and court costs, fees, copying, letters, paralegal fees, and anything else that you can think of.)
- A cost limit which can't be exceeded without your specific permission.
- Services you've agreed on.
- Process of paying bills including how to handle a retainer fee** if needed.
- Process of receiving itemized bills at regular intervals.
- Process for settling disputes.

**A retainer fee is a downpayment for services that will be performed. Get a receipt for the retainer fee if you pay one.

LEGAL CLINICS

Inexpensive legal clinics can sometimes be found. They are often located in shopping malls. They offer legal advice on such cases as landlord-tenant disputes, name changes, disability claims, contract reviews, and other simple legal advice. These clinics work in volume and have pre-set prices for specific services. Sometimes prices can be negotiated.

PREPAID LEGAL PLANS

There are legal plans that work like regular insurance. A fixed amount is paid per year even if you do not use the services. There are prepaid legal plans available on many campuses. Students need advice on such things as landlord/tenant disputes, traffic violations, crimes such as drug use or shoplifting, family law such as divorce or unplanned pregnancies, and insurance. Information will be available in the student offices.

SMALL CLAIMS COURT

Sometimes there are small problems that need to go to a small claims court for decisions. States set limits usually from $100 to $5,000. You should check with the small claims court in your area. The number can be found in the telephone directory listed under city or county court or clerk. You can also call the local county bar association. There is a small fee for filing the claim.

LEGAL AID OR PUBLIC DEFENDER

If you can't afford legal help on your own, there are federal agencies to help you. There may also be help through your local social and human services offices. Public Defenders usually represent indigent people who are facing jail sentences. Legal Aid offices help low income persons with legal fees for civil cases such as family, wage and rental disputes, and bankruptcy.

YOUR LEGAL RIGHTS

If you find yourself in jail, you will be asked a number of questions. You are required to give only your name and address. It is best to have a lawyer present before you answer further questions. Though you do have certain rights, your rights may be ignored. Your rights include:

- To be free from cruel and inhuman punishment.
- To be able to correspond with lawyers, courts, and legal-assistance agencies.
- To be free from sexual assault.
- To receive visitors.
- To receive health care and food.

CRIME VICTIM RIGHTS

There are programs to help a victim of a crime. Many states have victim/witness assistance programs available. You can find information about these programs in the telephone directory or you can place a call to the local police department, legal services agency, or the city or county clerk office. Victims, too, have rights:

- Not to be intimidated.
- To be told about agencies that offer assistance to crime victims.
- To be assisted by a local criminal justice agency.
- To be told about possible compensation.

SPIRITUAL SUPPORT

Since this is a time of exploration and setting your value system and personal goals, you might consider exploring your religious beliefs or disbeliefs. You can receive great personal and psychological support from a religious grounding. In addition to this, you can benefit from a large support base…an extended family.

Prepare for emergencies in your life before you have them! Religion can give you a foundation on which to build your value system and your life. It can help you through trying times.

You might try the church from which you received your basic training, if you had some. If you wish to explore other churches, look in the telephone directory and find other possibilities. You can call and find out what services are available to you. You can also call the minister, priest, rabbi, or other leader and make an appointment to talk. You will most likely be well received since people like to share their religious views and beliefs.

> Beware of religious cults. Research carefully any religion that attracts you. In any church, leaders should be accountable to some supervision. Young, idealistic, sincere individuals can have their faith exploited, often with tragic results. Brainwashing can occur in a short period of time so get information about groups. Be wary of overly warm, happy, or friendly groups or individuals who give vague answers, magical solutions and answers, and overemphasize how free you are to choose. If you are overwhelmed or lonely, talk to someone you know you can trust.

Formal Networks

There are formal networks such as businesses, associations, and clubs. Business and professional networks can assist in building a career through professional and community contacts. You will want to look for others who can help you to reach your career goals.

USING FORMAL AND INFORMAL NETWORKS TO FIND A JOB

If you want to find a job that might give you experience in the area in which you would like to work as a career, use a networking process.

•**List** all of the people whom you know that might help you. Include people from family friends, personal friends, parents of friends, teachers, church, activities, previous jobs, doctors, and relatives. (You should be able to list over 100.) From this list, choose about three people who would be able to tell you about the job areas in which you might be interested.

•**Contact** these persons, by phone, using the name of your contact person, and ask if they would be willing to meet with you for 15 minutes to give you some advice.

•**Prepare yourself:**
- List questions to ask about the career area in which you are interested.
- Put together a well written resume to show what you have done. (This may seem difficult if you have limited experience, but there are guides that can help you at the library.)
- Make plans to dress up in business type clothes when you get ready to make calls on your contacts. No matter what career you are hoping to have someday, dressing appropriately can offer the first impression that may get you a job. Borrow clothes if necessary.

•**When you go to the meeting,** inform the person that you are interested in the particular career that you have chosen, and that you understand that he/she can help to give you direction of the future of that business. Ask what training is best, what types of jobs help as you train for your career, etc. Let him/her know that you would value his/her advice. Before you leave, be sure to ask for the names of three other persons whom you might contact to see what they might suggest. Remember that you are only asking for advice and getting more names. Do not ask for a job!

•**Leave a resume** in case the persons know of an appropriate job. You will find that, if you make a good impression, they may even offer you a job themselves if they have one. If not, they may mention it to another colleague or remember you at a later time when they do have a job. People generally are flattered when asked for advice and enjoy helping a young person get started in an area in which they are interested.

•**Do NOT use this visit to ask for a job!** If the person is interested, he/she will make the first move.

•**Write a thank you note** to the person for his/her time.

•**Use the names** that you received from each person contacted and follow the same process. Your network grows and grows!

Moving Out

"How do I carry my 'stuff' to a new place?"

The amount of "stuff" you have to move helps dictate how it will be carried. Small amounts are usually done with a car or van. If there's a lot of "stuff," a trailer or van may be necessary. Doing it all yourself with help of friends is the least expensive way. Even if you have to rent a truck or van with a daily charge plus a cost per mile and insurance, it costs less than a mover.

Moving Yourself

MOVING WITH A TRAILER

- A car must have a trailer hitch on it to attach the trailer. A rental agency may have one to rent to you. Also check the trailer chain, brake lights, parking lights, and turn lights.
- Recheck the safety chain and hitch after you have driven it for 30 miles.
- If you rent a trailer, reserve the trailer in plenty of time ahead of the moving date.
- A trailer is difficult to back up and doesn't have much passing power. Drive carefully!
- Have the car serviced if you are going to be traveling very far and make sure it has enough power.

MOVING WITH A TRUCK OR VAN

- Check cost of insurance and mileage if you rent. Check exact return process to avoid extra charges.
- Make calls in advance of the rental date to make sure that the truck or van is available.
- Check to see if the vehicle has a stick shift. You may not have experience with one.
- Drive carefully. A truck is difficult to back up and there is less power than a car.

Preplanning Helps

What to do Before You Leave

- If you are moving out of town, close out old bank accounts and open new ones where you will move.
- Send out address changes (from post offices).

Include: credit card companies, draft board, magazine publishers, loan agencies, friends, insurance agents, and previous employer (for income tax form).
- Gather addresses of friends, your school, and your church. Ask persons to serve as references for you and take their addresses along too.
- Be sure to pick up any clothes that you have at a cleaners or laundry.

Prepare for Your New Occupancy

- Make calls, in advance, to hook up your gas, water, and electricity.
- Talk to your new landlord to get a guaranteed date of occupancy. Call a couple of days before you move to verify the date and see that the apartment has been cleaned or repaired as agreed. It is difficult to get things done once you move in.
- Be sure that someone will be there when you move in or that you have keys.

Plan for Your Valuables

- Gather all important papers and photographs so that they can be kept in a safe place: Social Security card, birth certificate, contracts, passport, glass prescriptions, medicine prescriptions, and immunization records. Don't depend on friends or movers. Take along doctor and dental records or get them sent ahead to your new doctor or dentist. (Ask for recommendations of new doctors where you are moving.)
- Professional movers are not generally liable for loss of valuables. Tend valuables **yourself.**
- Plan for plant and pet care. They're valuable too!

Plan Your Insurance

- Plan for rental insurance where you will be moving and during the time of the move. Read the small print and contact your insurance agent. You may need special moving insurance.

Gather Packing Supplies

- Start gathering packing supplies early. You can buy wardrobe and packing boxes from moving companies at a reasonable price. Watch for people moving in your neighborhood and ask to use their boxes when they've unpacked. Call ahead to grocery stores to ask when boxes will be available.
- Choose sturdy cardboard boxes that can be totally closed. Boxes the same size stack easily. Pack so they are carryable size with no more than 50 pounds.
- White paper, newsprint, paper towels, and tissue paper can be cut into packing size of 20"x 30" pieces. (Newsprint can damage some items because of the ink.)
- Try to find plastic bubble wrap for safe wrapping.
- Use a tape dispenser with heavy gummed tape to close boxes. You can also tape from the spool.
- Use black felt marker to mark what's in boxes and use color markers to show where boxes go.
- Find a furniture dolly to buy or to rent if you have heavy furniture or appliances to move.
- Find packing blankets to protect furniture. Moving or truck rental companies may rent some.

How to Pack

Avoid the rush and hectic days by packing early. Prepare a large surface with a blanket for packing. Place packing material items to be packed there. **Don't pack things that can cause damage if broken: shoe and furniture polish, nail polish remover, alcoholic beverages, aerosol cans, bleach.**

Packing Food

- Don't pack perishable foods unless they go quickly into safe storage.
- Nonperishable foods can freeze if they are out in weather. Tape shut opened boxes of food. Pack liquids inside plastic bags and seal tightly.
- Mark food boxes so that they can be easily distinguished. Move these boxes early if you can.

A packing no-no

Packing Cartons

- Wrap all items individually with clean paper. Newsprint is good packing material, but it can damage items with its ink. Use tissue paper, facial tissues, or paper towels to protect projected parts of delicate figurines and china. No sharp points or rims should be uncovered.
- Crush 2-3 inches of newspaper and pack it in bottom of box. Leave room for 2-3 inches at top too.
- Always put heaviest items in the bottom of the box. Continue packing with lightest things on top. The more fragile the item, the more cushioning is needed. Pillows and towels can add cushioning.
- Wind cords and fasten them so they won't dangle.
- Keep a written record of what is in each box. Number boxes so you know they've arrived.
- Close cartons securely with heavy tape or twine.
- Stack cartons together so they are ready to go and are out of the way. If you label with rooms where they will go, they can be packed together.
- Label all cartons with their contents. Label clearly on upper right-hand top, side, and end corners so that they can be read however they are placed. Write *FRAGILE This Side Up* on cartons containing any breakable items. You can mark boxes that should be unpacked first. Write your name on each box.

Packing Electronic Equipment

- Special care is needed for electronic equipment. Look at the owner's manual for special instructions. If possible use the original boxes. If you can't, pack each piece separately. Use tape to code wiring for easier installation. Allow time for equipment to return to room temperature before turning it on.

- **Personal computers** should have hard disk "Parked" using the program often included on the diagnostics diskette. The floppy disk drive can be protected by putting in an old or blank disk and closing the drive door. Back up any important disks.
- **Stereo/Compact Disc Players** should have stereo's tone arm fastened down. Tighten the turntable screws. Secure the dust cover so it won't move. A CD player needs special attention. First check the instructions to secure the laser. Do not move disks in a hot truck or van. Heat can warp compact disks.
- **TV/VCRs** should be treated as normal fragile items. Read any special instructions in the manual. Clean the VCR heads before you pack the VCR. Call cable personnel to see if they will connect the TV and VCR when you arrive if you plan cable. Tape a piece of cardboard over TV screen to protect it.

Packing Unusual Items

- **Awkward Items (i.e. bikes, tables)** should be disassembled. Keep pieces together. Attach screws or bolts to large pieces with tape or place in a plastic bag and tie on.
- **Records** should be packed on edge. Books should be packed flat.
- **Lightweight items from drawers** that can't be damaged through movement can be left there.
- **Small pictures and mirrors** should be wrapped individually in tissue paper or with towels or small blankets. Always place items on their edges. Small tacks or nails can be taped to the backs.

- **Lamp shades** should be placed in a box two inches larger than the shade. Pad the bottom of the box. Cover shade with clean paper. (No newspaper!) Nest other shades inside the shade if they don't touch each other. Silk shades can rip or stretch. Don't place crushed paper around the shade.

How To Load

- When loading a trailer or truck, pack the heaviest things first and lowest. Do just one fourth of the truck at a time. Fill from the bottom to the top. Tie each section firmly with a rope to avoid shifting.
- Carefully look to see that nothing has been left behind.
- Clean up after you've moved out. If you are leaving an apartment, you could leave a packet of instructions for items such as appliances and furnace, information about the neighborhood, flowers and/or wine. **Wow! Wouldn't you like to see your new apartment or room delivered to YOU that way?**

Other Hints

- A "fix-it-box" of tools that will be needed when you unpack could be prepared ahead of time. Include:
  hammer
  light bulbs
  hot pot or small pan for heating water or soups
  flashlight
  toilet paper
  snacks, paper plates, cups, silverware
  paper towels and rags for cleaning
  bucket
  retractable knife for opening boxes
- Don't move things you won't use. Have a rummage sale or donate articles for tax deductions.
- Prepare a special box for last minute items: cosmetics, toothbrushes, toilet tissue, toilet paper, towels.
- Plan a rain plan. Borrow or rent a tarpaulin to tie on the top of trailer. Fasten well!

MOVING IN...THINGS TO WATCH

- Don't start a fire in a fireplace without checking it. Packing papers and boxes invite chimney fires.
- Check to find how things work. Check appliances, furnace, locks, and windows. Find the fuse box.
- Find out who your neighbors are. If they don't come to meet you, go to meet them. You need to know someone immediately in case of emergency.

When Using Professional Movers

Most people starting out can't afford professional movers. If you want to find costs, shop around. Ask for references from friends and family. Check with the Better Business Bureau. Call at least two or three companies before you choose. Companies generally send someone without cost to your home to give estimates and tell you about the services. Ask about services, advance charges, appliance service, estimates (including binding estimates), insurance costs, and how payment is made. Moving companies often give literature to help with planning and preplanning.

Know the Terms

- A **binding estimate** clearly describes the shipment and all services provided. You can't be required to pay any more than the amount of the estimate. This estimate must be in writing and a copy given to you before you move. A copy must also be attached to the bill of lading.
- A **non-binding estimate** of approximate cost does not bind the mover to the estimate that is given. There is no guarantee that the final cost will not be more than the estimate. Check to see how much must be paid when the delivery is made.
- An **order of service** is not a contract. You should get a copy of this when it is prepared. Be sure to notify the company if there are any changes of dates or if you have decided not to use the services. Any changes to be made must be prepared in writing. Get a written copy of the changes.

- A **bill of lading** is a contract between you and the mover. The information included on this paper is the same information given on the order for service. It is required by law. Get a copy from the driver who loads your shipment. You must sign this then. Be sure to read everything before you sign! Do no lose or misplace your copy!
- The **shipment is weighed** so that charges can be made. This is generally done at the place of origin.
- **Insurance** must be carefully considered to see if any losses will be paid for by replacement value, by weight, or by its present value. You should also consider the amount of insurance that is available through your rental or household insurance. Check to see if there is coverage when you move. (A fur coat, if lost, could return to you as $5.00 or less if judged by weight.)

If You Have Trouble With the Move

The Interstate Commerce Commission (ICC) regulates interstate moves. If you have any concerns, you can contact ICC's offices of Compliance and Consumer Assistance (OCCA). If you want information, contact the headquarters office:

Room 4133
Interstate Commerce Commission Bldg.
12th Street and Constitution Avenue, N.W.
Washington, DC 20423

Looking Good

"How can I build an appropriate wardrobe and take care of it?"

When starting out on your own you can create a whole new image of yourself. Your only limitations are what you already own, what resources you have, and your knowledge about clothing. Clothing helps to create the image.

Five Step Clothing Plan

#1 Think through your personality and the messages you want to send with your clothes.

Through your own observations, you have understandings of the messages that clothing sends. (i.e. "I want to join your group." "I value style." "I'm quiet." "I'm a leader." "I'm looking for a mate." "I want to be successful in business." "I don't care what you think!") What image do you want to create? Is clothing important enough to make the effort to plan?

#2 Review your goals. Consider the type of clothing that will help you to get there.

If your long term goals require many dollars to accomplish, you may have to be very economical with your clothing dollar as you work toward the goals. This will take efficient planning if you also wish to create an image of prosperity and organizational ability.

#3 Gather information about clothes that are appropriate and costs involved.

If you are headed to school away from home, find out what is worn on campus. You can go to see or you can ask someone who goes there. If you go directly to a job, research appropriate clothing for what you will be doing.

If you want to "look good" with the clothes you wear, line, design, and color can help you. They can create optical illusions to "fool the eye." They can make you appear thinner, heavier, taller, shorter, or whatever you would like to be!

LINE & DESIGN

Eyes actually follow lines that they see. You can create lines to your advantage.

Want to Look Shorter?

Create a line that carries the eye horizontally. (Wear contrasting colors such as shirt of white and pants of navy blue. Wear clothes with lines created from trimmings and seams that go horizontally.)

Want to Look Taller?

Create lines that carry the eye vertically. (Wear clothes of the same color, even carrying out the same color in stockings and shoes if you can. Use vertical lines created from trimmings and design details such as pockets, buttons, seams, and trimmings.)

Want to Look Thinner?

Wear dark, plain colors. Wear vertical lines in trim, design details, and seam design. Use light or medium weight fabrics. All one color from head to toe is helpful. Avoid contrasting tops and bottoms, wide waistbands, and contrasting belts.

Want to Look Heavier?

Wear lighter colors. Wear horizontal lines in trim, design, and seams. You can also wear loose fitting clothes so your size is not so apparent. Fabrics that have designs on them can also make you appear heavier. Large people should wear large designs. Small people should wear smaller designs. Bulky fabrics or loosely fitted clothing help too.

Want to Change the Size of Different Areas of Your Body?

If there is a part of your body that you want to appear to be a different size, try the same principles. Attract the eye to the areas you want to make larger with horizontal lines. If you want the area to appear smaller, keep the eye away from the area and carry out vertical lines. (Examples: If you want broader shoulders, wear contrasting colors at the shoulder line to carry the eye sideways. If you have broad ankles, wear simple shoes designed to make you look straight up the leg, not across the foot. For making a forehead look wider, wear bangs. A narrow chin invites curls at the chin area.)

COLORS

There is a definite psychology of colors. There is also a reflection and contrast to your skin tones that can or cannot flatter you.

What colors show my personality?

Greens and blues remind us of living, growing things and calm, blue waters. Reds, yellows, and oranges remind us of fire, sun, and energy. Navy blues remind us of military discipline. Black reminds us of night and mystery. Browns make us think of tree trunks and earth. Density of a color says things too. A quiet, shy person may be most comfortable in pale, cool, neutral colors. A dramatic, vivacious person may prefer to wear bright, bold colors.

What colors look good on me?

Color illusions can change the way you appear to others. There are some colors that make your skin look clearer and healthier. Body size and shape, hair, and eye color can be improved. Some colors are unflattering too. Bright color draws attention to a part of the body. This is a good way to draw attention to your good body features (i.e. a scarf, tie, or jewelry close to the face can draw attention there).

Analyze what looks best on you by thinking about outfits that you wear when people compliment you. Place colors close to your face and see what the reflections of the colors do to your skin tones. You can also get a color analysis by someone trained in the techniques or you can read about colors and analyze yourself. *Color Me Beautiful* by Carole Jackson offers detailed information for your own personal color analysis.

#4 Review Your Budget

Take a hard look at your budget to see how much you can actually afford to spend on clothing. If you feel the need is greater than what you can afford, consider alternative ways to pay for what you need.

WAYS TO SAVE DOLLARS

Recycle

- Cut off legs of jeans or pants to make shorts.
- Cover holes with iron-on appliques or patches if holes are out of style.
- Modify garments to meet current styles:
  - Straighten legs or full skirts by removing fullness.
  - Change buttons.
  - Shorten garment if hemlines are shorter.
  - Remove or add shoulder pads.
  - Make wide neckties narrower.
  - Use new accessories.
  - Cut jeans that are too short and make into a bag.
  - Make long sleeves into short ones.

Sew If You Can

If you have the capability of sewing your own clothes, you can save many dollars if you plan carefully.

- Price fabrics for clothes you sew since they can sometimes cost more than purchased clothing.
- Use recycled buttons for trim.
- Remake your old garments or clothes from rummage sales and resale shops.
- Use new or old tablecloths, drapes, bedspreads, or sheets.
- Use fabric pieces to create patchwork designs.

Shop in Unusual Places

Shop in thrift shops, outlet stores, mission stores, rummage sales, antique stores, garage sales, resale stores, Goodwill, and consignment stores. Look in newspaper want ads. Search different store departments for such things as jackets, shirts, sneakers, and sweaters. Clothes from various departments may fit you and prices do vary. Sportswear and lingerie sections may have items that are appropriate for different occasions. Be wary of low cost merchandise sold out of temporary quarters such as motels and parking lots. Merchandise may be stolen or of poor quality.

Preplan!

- Analyze your needs and your wants. See what your budget allows and plan carefully.
- List the things that you really need before you go shopping. Buy only what's on the list.

- Avoid buying on credit. If you choose to put clothes on "lay-away," check the added costs and the process if you would change your mind about the purchase.
- Limit your wardrobe. The more clothes you have, the more work you have for their care and storage.
- Consider choosing basic styles and add distinctive accessories to give you the variety that you desire.
- Choose the basic colors of your wardrobe and stick to them! This offers a variety of mix and match.
- Buy clothes that are considered classics (i.e. blazers, cardigan sweaters, shirtwaist dresses, white shirts, loafer shoes, and simple lines that have been "in" for years) since they stay in style and are versatile.
- Buy garments that can be worn during most seasons of the year.
- Look at current fashions and do comparison shopping. Don't buy fads that go out of style quickly.
- Choose the quality appropriate for the length of time to be used and the durability necessary.

Added Money Savers

- Check if an item can be returned, the time limit allowed, and if there's a cash or credit on returns.
- If an item's defective, return it as soon as possible. Be sure that you followed label directions.
- Take care of what you buy. Repair as needed. Keep things clean, and use proper cleaning methods.
- Consider delivery costs of catalog and television orders. There could be delivery costs for returns too.
- Read care labels to know if you can take care of clothing without dry-cleaning.
- Be aware of fabric characteristics so that you get the durability that you want (i.e. acrylics "pill").
- Buy on sale, but be careful that you avoid buying just because it is a bargain.
- Try on before you buy, especially if there is no return policy on the item.

Know Shopping Vocabulary

- **First quality**—perfect condition.
- **Irregular**—slight flaw.
- **Second**—more flawed than an irregular. Examine items carefully!
- **Sale**—regular prices are reduced for a limited time.
- **Clearance**—regular store merchandise is being sold at lower price to reduce stock of store.
- **Odd lots**—usually first quality of left-over merchandise after retailers order.
- **Overstock**—overruns of first quality merchandise that is left after retailers have ordered.
- **Discontinued, canceled goods**—may be first, irregular, or second quality that is no longer produced.
- **Samples**—merchandise that was shown to buyers before their orders were taken.
- **Special purchase**—merchandise not normally sold by the store. Watch out for inferior merchandise.
- **Warehouse sale**—merchandise is sold out of a warehouse at lower than normal prices.
- **Introductory offer**—limited time price reduction. Items will be sold at higher prices later.
- **Returns**—merchandise that has been returned by customers or retailers.
- **Comparable value**—can be misleading. Do comparison shopping to check the claim.

Special Thrift Store Shopping Hints

- Check under arms, around the neck, and down the back for signs of wear.
- Check for tiny holes by holding garment up to light. (Moth and silver fish holes may not be visible.)
- Check seams by pulling gently to see if the fabric is durable and not rotting. (Silks are very fragile.)
- Some fabrics that say "dry-clean" may be washable with careful handling. Most silks and wools can be washed in cold water soap. Clothes needing extensive pressing, such as suits, should be dry-cleaned.
- Wool sweaters can be shrunk by washing in cold water soap and drying in the dryer. Remove

before fully dry and stretch to block to the size you want. Lay flat to dry.

- Look carefully for spots.
- Don't buy clothes with an odor. Even after dry-cleaning, odors can return.

#5 Make a Clothing Plan

The things that you already have are the basis for your future wardrobe. As you analyze each item, consider if you really like it, if you want to replace it, or if you wish to dispose of it. If you want to get rid of it, consider selling it at a resale shop, flea market, consignment store, or donating it.

As you plan, consider how items can be coordinated to create new outfits and how accessories can make different looks. Also plan appropriateness of clothes for your activities. Look at your near future goals to consider additions that can be used now and also in the future. Plan for the changeover.

After you are finished with the inventory, prioritize what is needed most and least. Number them in the order of your needs. Also think about what is a <u>need</u> and what is a <u>want</u>.

WARDROBE INVENTORY

Money Available for Purchasing Clothes $ _____

Description of Usable Clothes	Cost of Cleaning and Repair	Description of Apparel Needed	Date Needed	Estimated Cost	Actual Cost
Pants					
Sport Shirts/ Blouses					
Skirts					
Dresses					
Blazers/Jackets					

Description of Usable Clothes	Cost of Cleaning and Repair	Description of Apparel Needed	Date Needed	Estimated Cost	Actual Cost
Dress shirts/ Blouses					
Shorts					
Sweaters					
Coats					
Athletic attire					
Shoes/boots					
Underwear					
Socks					
Sleepwear					
Neckwear/ Scarves					
Jewelry					
Hats/gloves					
Belts					
Other things					
Total costs	$			$	$

Hungry? Eat Healthy?

"How can I feed myself and stay healthy?"

Eating only what you like can spell poor health. Unfortunately results of poor eating habits do not show up instantly. They sneak up as dull hair, scaly skin, weight gain or weight loss, "zits," lack of energy, illness…eventually causing more serious problems in later life.

Food is like an insurance policy. When your body receives the right chemicals (yes, you are really a chemical factory!), you tend to stay healthier throughout your life. You look better. You produce healthier children. You are more able to use your body to its best advantage. You not only look better and feel better now but you'll look better and feel better when you're "old"!

Making Healthy Food Choices

Food scientists have studied how bodies use food. Keeping track of each food and nutrient is complicated. To make it easier, nutritionists created The Food Guide Pyramid to replace the time-honored Basic Four Food Plan used worldwide to help people get the chemicals (nutrients) they need. There are also new dietary guidelines.

Food Choice Guidance

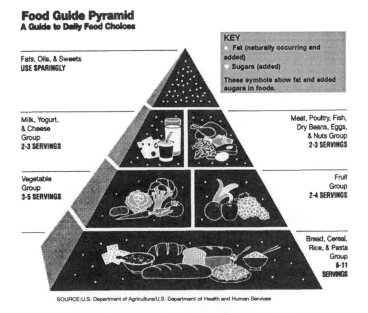

Food Guide Pyramid
A Guide to Daily Food Choices

Fats, Oils, & Sweets
USE SPARINGLY

KEY
○ Fat (naturally occurring and added)
▽ Sugars (added)
These symbols show fat and added sugars in foods.

Milk, Yogurt, & Cheese Group
2-3 SERVINGS

Meat, Poultry, Fish, Dry Beans, Eggs, & Nuts Group
2-3 SERVINGS

Vegetable Group
3-5 SERVINGS

Fruit Group
2-4 SERVINGS

Bread, Cereal, Rice, & Pasta Group
6-11 SERVINGS

SOURCE:U.S. Department of Agriculture/U.S. Department of Health and Human Services

Dietary Guidelines for Americans

The newest dietary guidelines prepared for the U.S.* include the following:

1. Eat a variety of foods. Use foods from the base of the pyramid as a foundation of meals. Choose a variety of foods from each of the five food groups.

2. Balance the food you eat with physical activity. Maintain or improve your weight. If overweight, try to lose, or at least, not gain weight. Balance amount of calories in foods and drinks with the amount of calories the body uses. Try to do 30 minutes or more of exercise each day.

3. Choose a diet with plenty of grain products, vegetables, and fruits. Eat dry beans, lentils, and peas more often. Increase fiber intake with more whole grains, whole grain products, dry beans, fiber-rich vegetables and fruits (i.e. carrots, corn, peas, pears, and berries).

4. Choose a diet low in fat, saturated fat, and cholesterol. Consume no more than a total of 30% of fat in your diet. Only 10% of the fat intake should come from saturated fats found mostly in meat, milk, palm oil, and coconut oil. The rest of the fat should be from polyunsaturated and monosaturated fats found in vegetable oils, nuts, and high-fat fish. Partially hydrogenated vegetable oils, such as those used in some margarines and shortenings, contain a form of unsaturated fat that may raise blood cholesterol levels, although not as much as saturated fat. Animal products are the only source of cholesterol in your diet. The upper limit on the grams of fat in your diet will depend on the calories you need. Example:

MAXIMUM TOTAL FAT INTAKE AT DIFFERENT CALORIE LEVELS

Calories	1,600	2,200	2,800
Total Fat	53	73	93

5. Choose a diet moderate in sugars. Avoid excessive snacking. Brush teeth with fluoride tooth paste. Floss regularly.

6. Choose a diet moderate in salt and sodium. Eat less than 2,400 mg of salt per day. (l level teaspoon salt = 2,300 g of sodium.)

7. If you drink alcoholic beverages, do so in moderation. No more than 1/day for women and 2/day for men. Count as drinks:

12 oz regular beer (150 calories)

5 oz wine (100 calories)

1.5 oz 80 proof distilled spirits (100 calories)

People who should not drink:
- Children, adolescents
- Individuals who can't restrict drinking to moderate levels (especially recovering alcoholics or people whose family members have alcohol problems)
- Women trying to conceive or are pregnant
- Individuals who plan to drive or take part in activities that require attention or skill
- Individuals using prescriptions or over-counter drugs

*Adapted from Home and Garden Bulletin #232 4th Edition, 1995 U.S. Dept. of Agriculture, U.S. Department of Health and Human Services

Water is Healthy Too!

There are definite health benefits of water. Water acts as a building material of cells and tissues, carries nutrients, removes waste products, helps digestion, lubricates joints, and regulates temperature. It is important! **Eight glasses of liquid a day are recommended.**

Dieting

You might question, "But, won't I get fat eating all that is recommended?" The answer is "NO." You must, however, choose foods that you need and be careful to avoid foods that have a high calorie count, usually from fats and sugars. There is only one way of dieting that is successful over the long run. This method combines eating fewer calories and exercising more.

> **Eat foods that supply nutrients your body needs to function efficiently.**

Review the Food Pyramid to see what your body needs. (If the recommended amounts seem like there will be too much food to eat to lose weight, reconsider!) You can get a healthful diet of about 1100 calories by cutting the fat and sugar additives.

MEDIAN HEIGHTS AND WEIGHTS AND RECOMMENDED ENERGY INTAKE

Category	Age (years)	Weight	Height	Per day*
Males	15-18	145	69	3,000
	19-24	160	70	2,900
	25-50	174	70	2,900
	51+	170	68	2,300
Females	15-18	120	64	2,200
	19-24	128	65	2,200
	25-50	138	64	2,200
	51+	143	63	1,900

*In the range of light to moderate activity
(Taken from *Recommended Dietary Allowances 10th Edition* National Research Council)

There is no exact answer to what the correct weight is for you, but you can try to follow suggested weights for adults:

Height	Weight in pounds for 19-34 year olds*
5'0"	97-128
5'1"	101-132
5'2"	104-137
5'3"	107-141
5'4"	111-146
5'5"	114-150
5'6"	118-155
5'7"	121-160
5'8"	125-164
5'9"	129-169
5'10"	132-174
5'11"	136-179
6'0"	140-184
6'1"	144-189
6'2"	148-195
6'4"	156-205
6'5"	160-211

*Higher weights generally apply to men because they have more muscle and bone. Lower weights generally apply to women because they have less muscle and bone.

A SIMPLE WAY TO KEEP TRACK OF CALORIES

One simple way to keep track of your calories is to judge by the following general guide of the amount of calories in each of the food groups. These simple averages can help you keep track easily.

Food Group	Size of Serving	Calories of Low Calorie Foods	Calories of Higher Calorie Foods
Milk	1 cup	85 (skim)	150 (whole)
Vegetables	1/2 cup	30 (non starchy)*	70 (starchy)*
Fruits	1 piece or 1/2 cup	60	80
Bread/cereal	1 piece or 1 cup	60 (bread)	100 (cereal)
Meat	2 to 3 ounces**	150 (lean)	250 (more fat)
Others (i.e. candy, pastries)	Too much!	Even more!	Worse yet!!

*Starchy vegetables include such things as potatoes, peas, and corn. Non starchy vegetable examples are: broccoli, lettuce, green beans, cauliflower, and carrots.

**2 or 3 ounces of meat is about the size of a deck of cards.

By using the above chart you can see that eating the least requirements for you as suggested in the Food Pyramid can cut calories to less than 1200 per day. These calories are based on low fat food choices (i.e. skim milk, chicken breast, non-starchy vegetables **not** milk shakes, T-bone steak, and French fries!).

2 milk=	170 calories
3 vegetables=	90 calories
2 fruits=	120 calories
2 meat=	300 calories
6 cereal=	360 calories
Total...	**1,040 calories**

These 1,040 calories may not be enough calories to keep you going at your best. Your caloric requirement may be higher, especially if you are active and large. (See charts.) It will, however, give you the nutrients that you need. This type of diet doesn't allow fat seasonings or sugars on your foods. Each time you add these, you add calories. You can see from this illustration that you can cut calories if you have the discipline and the desire.

> A quick, easy way of *estimating* the number of calories you eat each day is to count each item eaten and multiply by 100. This method only averages, but is a general way of keeping track with reasonable accuracy. If you need to be more accurate, follow the above plan or use a food calorie guide.

Do's for Calorie Cutting!

- **Do** figure the number of calories that you need per day.
- **Do** increase the number of pastas and bread eaten. WATCH fat content added in sauces, cheese, and butter.
- **Do** use 100% whole grain bread which includes minerals, bulk, and Vitamin E.
- **Do** drink skim milk and use low fat products.
- **Do** eat lean meats such as fish, white turkey, or chicken breasts. (Remove fat and skins.)
- **Do** remember that potatoes are a nutritious vegetable, not a bread or cereal. Limit gravy, fats, and creams.
- **Do** figure the number of fat calories that you should not exceed. Figure that there are 9 calories in 1 gram of fat. If you want to figure more accurately: 100 lb. person x 15 calories per pound = 1500 calories. (30% of 1500 = 450 calories from fat divided by 9 calories per gram =50 grams of fat per day.)

- **Do** exercise at least 30 minutes a day. (Walk and climb stairs in between!)
- **Do** get as much information as you can from the places you eat and/or from a nutrition book.
- **Do** eat small amounts of low fat and low calorie salad dressings. Get dressing served "on the side" if eating out or dip forkful of salad into dressing instead of putting dressing directly on salad.
- **Do** cut cravings by tasting very small amounts of things not on the "good food" list once in a while.

Don'ts for Calorie Cutting!

- **Don't** remove bread from your diet! You need the B vitamins in it. Use little margarine or butter.
- **Don't** eat fried foods. (Goodbye, French fries!)
- **Don't** eat extra fat in your diet. (Limit salad dressings, butters, and margarines)
- **Don't** drink regular sodas and alcoholic beverages. (They have calories too!)
- **Don't** eat sweets such as candies, donuts, cakes, and pies.

Other Suggestions for Calorie Cutting

Dieting can be difficult if you don't like fruits and vegetables, or if you can't prepare your own food.

- If you can't get the fruits and vegetables you need where you eat, stop at a grocer's and buy some to store in your own room. Instead of fatty snacks, eat these in addition to your regular foods.
- Drink fruit juices and water instead of sodas. Some diet sodas have no calories, but do have additives that may cause health problems. They are very expensive and have no nutritional value. Regular sodas contain only sugar and no other nutrients.
- Since pizzas are high in fat, choose one with vegetables and low calorie mozzarella cheese toppings.
- Avoid processed meats such as hot dogs and sandwich meats.
- Eat low fat, low salt snacks. Keep them in your room or carry them along.
- Read labels and ask for nutritional information at fast food restaurants.

Watch Out for Fast Foods

Fast foods have a reputation as unhealthy foods. Fortunately, there are also good nutrients in most of the foods. Unfortunately, fast foods do contain a great deal of fat, calories, and sodium (salt). There is very little calcium and vitamin A and C that are necessary to balance a diet. As an example, a quarter-pound cheeseburger, large fries, and vanilla shake can add up to over half of your needs per day!

Calories = 1,205   Fat = 59 grams   Sodium = 1,655 milligrams

Chicken and fish sandwiches, that you may consider lower in calories and fats, are comparatively higher than a plain hamburger because of the fat in which the meat is fried. Most fast food restaurants do have nutritional information. Request it.

Tips on Eating Fast Foods

If you are concerned about your weight, if you are concerned about possible heart problems because of fat and salt in your diet, or if you want to get a balanced diet while eating often at fast food restaurants, consider these tips:

1. Choose smaller sized sandwiches without extra cheese, bacon, and sauces.

2. Order roast beef if you want leaner meat. (Lean beef has fewer fat grams than many sandwiches such as deep fried chicken with sauces and skin, and/or fatty hamburgers.)

3. Avoid breaded, deep fat fried chicken and fish sandwiches. Beware of chicken nuggets.

4. Choose to eat as many vegetables as you can from a salad bar or from the fixings on a sandwich.

5. If there are no baked potatoes available, choose a small order of French fries without salt added.

6. If you choose baked or mashed potatoes, add cream, butter, and/or margarine sparingly.

7. If you order chicken with a choice of biscuit or roll, choose the roll. Most biscuits have saturated fat.

8. Avoid heavy use of dressings if you are eating salads.

9. Drink low fat milk instead of sodas or shakes. Water has no calories, fat, or salt, or cost!

10. Most desserts are full of calories and fats, so avoid them when possible.

11. Buy fruits and vegetables and healthy snacks to fill in your diet with the missing nutrients.

Food Additives

Have you wondered if additives in your food are safe for you to eat? You are going to have to decide if you are going to worry about them or not. Many additives are familiar things such as salt, sugar, vanilla, and yeast. Other additives are complex chemical compounds used to extend our food supply. They are used to: preserve; improve taste, texture, consistency, and color; improve nutritional quality; provide leavening; control acidity/alkalinity. Additives in this country are carefully controlled by the FDA (Food and Drug Administration). Any substance that is added to food has been carefully researched before approval. New additives or substitutes are being created all the time. Watch for information about them. Many are not yet proven. Another thing not considered with additives is the effect they have when put together with others in foods. Some additives used in food processing that cause concern are:

- Sodium nitrate and sodium nitrite used to preserve processed meats (i.e. ham, luncheon meats, hot dogs, and sausage.)
- BHA and BHT used to keep such foods as bread fresh.

> **Use as few foods as possible that have chemical additives in them.**

Read the Labels!

Food labels were created to clear up confusion in advertising and also to help consumers improve their diets. Don't be fooled with labels promising such things as "Low fat," "Light," "No Cholesterol"! Labeling laws will help you judge. They are required on almost all packages except for restaurant and medical foods, coffee, tea, and spices with few nutrients, and foods sold by vendors.

Labels must include a listing of ingredients. They are to be listed by weight, with the heaviest ingredient first and the rest in descending order. You may read on a label: *Ingredients: water, pineapple juice, apple juice, sugar.* This means that there is more water than pineapple juice, apple juice, or sugar. The amounts of the ingredients do not need to be listed.

Serving Sizes on Labels

Labels are standardized. They are based on national surveys that consider what an average person actually eats at each sitting. As an example, fruits and vegetables are usually listed as 1/2 cup per serving. A meat serving for single-ingredient raw meat and poultry is 3 ounces.

There is one thing to remember. If one unit weighs more than 50% but less than 200% of the standardized amount, then the serving size equals one unit. This means, as an example, that a soda's standardized amount is 8 ounces. A 12-ounce serving is considered only one serving even though its calorie amount increases 50%!

Nutrient Claims on Labels

Nutrient claims made by businesses must follow guidelines. Here are definitions to help.

FREE, WITHOUT, NO, or ZERO: Product contains no (or almost no) fat, cholesterol, sodium, sugars, or calories. (A calorie-free product can't contain more than five calories per serving.)

FRESH: Applies only to raw or unprocessed foods. Product has never been frozen or heated and contains no preservatives.

FRESH FROZEN: Used for foods that are quickly frozen while fresh.

GOOD SOURCE: One serving of a food contains 10 to 19% of Daily Value of a nutrient per reference amount.

HIGH SOURCE: Contains 20% or more of the Daily Value of a particular nutrient in one serving.

JUICE: Made of 100% juice. Other products must tell the percentage of juices and be called other names such as "juice beverage" or "juice drink."

LEAN or EXTRA LEAN: Describes fat content of meat, poultry, game, and seafood. Measurements are given in per 100 g servings: Lean: less than 10 g fat, less than 4 g saturated fat, less than 95 mg cholesterol. Extra lean: less than 5 g fat, less than 2 g saturated fat, less than 95 mg cholesterol.

LESS: Contains 25% less of a nutrient or of calories than the reference food.

LIGHT or LITE: Applied only to calories, fat, and sodium. For calories and fat, *light* means that the food has one-third fewer calories or half the fat of a reference food. For sodium, *Light* means the sodium content must be reduced at least 50%. *Light* can also refer to food attributes such as color and texture. The foods must be similar to the product it represents such as regular potato chips compared to *Light* potato chips.

LOW: Food can be eaten frequently without exceeding dietary guidelines for fat, cholesterol, sodium, or calories.

MORE: Serving of food, altered or not, contains at least 10% more of a nutrient than the Daily Value of the reference food.

% FAT FREE: Reflects the amount of fat present in 100 g of a low-fat or fat-free product. A percentage will be reflected.

REDUCED: Contains 25% less of a nutrient or of calories than the regular reference product. Any product that already meets this rule may not claim it is *Reduced.*

SUGAR FREE: Contains less than 0.5 g of sugar per reference amount and has no added sugars or ingredients containing sugar.

VERY LOW SODIUM: Contains no more than 35 mg per reference amount and per 50 g if reference amount is less than or equal to 30 g or 2 tablespoons.

I FEEL AWFUL!!

**Converting Grams and Ounces
When Reading Labels**

- 1 pound (lb) = 454 grams (g)
- 1 ounce (oz) = 28 grams (g)
- 1 gram = 1,000 milligrams (mg)
- 1 milligram = 1,000 micrograms (mcg)

Eat In or Eat Out Choices

When you are considering whether you should eat out most of the time or cook at home, consider what each way will cost, what you are capable of, and if you have equipment and knowledge to cook and stay healthy. This section will help make the decision.

Eating Out

Dormitory Food

Dormitory food can be your answer if you are on a campus where this is available. Sorority and fraternity houses usually have food served at the houses. Sometimes meal plans are available that do not include all meals. In this case, a compromise of eating on your own, even in the dorm room, can be the answer.

Fast Food Restaurants

Fast foods are a favorite because they can be reasonably priced and convenient. You don't have to make reservations. You save time. You don't have to tip. Though fast foods are often considered "junk" foods, they do have essential nutrients which include proteins, and **some** vitamins and minerals. Many restaurants furnish nutrition information so you can make healthy choices. Compare the cost of eating in a fast food restaurant and an inexpensive family restaurant. The difference may be small.

Family Restaurants

A family restaurant has many different types of motifs and menus. You have enough variety to order a balanced meal that you like. Following are some general suggestions that will help you when eating out.

Menus:

- A menu is often posted at the entrance so you can think ahead. It shows food available and costs.

- Ala carte foods which are priced individually are usually more expensive.
- Note what is offered with each menu choice. If you can't tell by reading, ask.
- Ask if there are smaller portions or half portions available if you want less or want to share. There may be a charge for an extra plate. You can also take leftover food home.
- Choose a balanced meal.

Save Dollars

- Order water for a beverage. Drinks are expensive. There's little food value in coffee or soda.
- Order "Special of the Day." It is freshly prepared and usually more reasonable. Check prices.
- Desserts and appetizers can be shared with your dinner partner but may not be worth the price.
- If the food is not well prepared, send it back. (Don't eat most of it first!)

Check Your Check

- Be sure to check your bill carefully. Call errors to attention of waiter/waitress.
- For tipping, check bill to see if gratuity has been added. Figure tip only on cost of meal, not tax.

Fancy Restaurants

- Check ahead to see if reservations are needed, and if there is a dress code, what it is.
- Plan to arrive on time. If you are going to be late or want to cancel your reservation, call.
- Ask the waiter/waitress about what you don't understand on the menu. You can also ask what is included in the entree (main course). Very often if foods are ordered ala carte, the entree is a meal in itself which includes vegetables. Ask any questions that will help you with your ordering.
- If you have a special request such as broiled meat and little salt or fat, ask if you can be accommodated.
- If the food is poorly prepared, return it. You are paying for good quality and should receive it.
- Always be polite.
- Tipping is expected. See if the tip (gratuity) has

been added to the bill. Figure tip on food, not tax. The host/hostess is usually not tipped. The tip must also cover extra people waiting on you like a wine steward. The acceptable amount is at least 15% of the bill.

- Check over your bill carefully. If there is an error, quietly ask the waiter/waitress to explain.

Menu Terms

Menus can be very confusing if you don't know the terms. It's a good idea to learn at least the main terms to protect yourself and to avoid questioning the waiter/waitress. Some terms most frequently seen on menus include the following:

A la carte	Each menu item ordered and priced separately
Antipasto	Assorted Italian relishes
Appetizers	Assorted small foods served to stimulate the appetite before meals
Aperitif	A mild, alcoholic beverage served at the beginning a meal to increase appetite
Au gratin	Sprinkled with crumbs and/or cheese, then baked until brown
Au jus	Served with natural juice or gravy
Bearnaise sauce	A hollandaise sauce with vinegar or wine, shallots, and tarragon
Chataubriand	Thick piece of beef filet served with bearnaise sauce (usually prepared for two people)
Coq au vin	French preparation of chicken, cooked in red wine sauce
Du jour	"Of the day," a special offering (i.e. soup du jour available that day)
Entree	American main course or French course served before the main course
Flambe	Food served after flaming with brandy or liquor
Fondu Bourguignon	Small pieces of meat that are deep fried at the table
Fondu Suisse	Melted cheese with white wine and kirsch in which bread cubes are dipped
Hollandaise	A sauce made with eggs, oil, and seasonings
Jardiniere or La jardiniere	Meat or poultry served with fresh cooked vegetables
Mousse	Light delicate dish made with gelatin
Newberg sauce	Creamy sauce used for lobster or shrimp
Parfait	Layered dessert including ice cream, whipped cream, sauces, and syrups (served in tall container)
Pasta	All forms of macaroni
Pate	Ground, seasoned meat or meats served with or without pastry coverings
Quiche Lorraine	Unsweetened custard and bacon tart
Ragout	Highly seasoned stew served with meat and vegetables
Sashimi	Raw fish dipped in sauces, usually served as an appetizer
Table d'hote	A fixed price for all the courses of a meal
Vichyssoise	A cream soup usually made of leeks and potatoes and served cold

Eating In

Eating at home has many advantages. You don't have to dress up. You have more choices and can cook what you like. You can save money. You can use it as a hobby to express yourself. It also has disadvantages. You have to plan the meals and shop for the food. You have to take time to cook and clean up. It requires equipment. It can be lonely. You have to have knowledge to cook well.

Thanks to technological advances, eating at home may be your best choice. There are time-saving foods available in the market place. Very often, however, there are many additives in the foods to keep them preserved and tasting good. Some of the fiber needed by your body, and some nutrients may be missing. Many of these foods cost more money.

You will find many labor-saving devices as you practice. You may find that freezing meals can be very time saving. When you cook a big meal, make extra to freeze. Plan to cook extra so you won't have to cook another night. Some people even like to cook just one day and then eat the extra frozen food they prepared the rest of the week. Just be sure that you cool and freeze food quickly so there will be no food poisoning for you later in the week!

Grazing

"Grazing" has become a way of life for many families...just like the animals living off the grassy fields, they just keep eating small amounts all day long. This can be a very effective way to keep your energy level, but it can also be dangerous when the wrong foods are chosen. Many of our snack foods contain much fat, much salt, many calories, and few nutrients. Foods chosen well can, however, meet your needs.

- Read the required nutrition labels on the snacks and choose wisely.
- Plan your snacks.
- Keep the basic foods of the Food Pyramid in mind when you choose.
- Be sure that the fat content of the foods does not have more calories than 30% of your diet.
- Keep nutritious, "transportable" snacks available where you are:

small cans of juice	fresh fruits
crackers	nuts
pretzels	cereals
cheese cubes	small pieces of meat
milk	popcorn
prepared fresh vegetables	dried fruits
yogurt	"trail mix"

- If you really crave sweets, use small size candy bars and popsicles. If you can, make your own popsicles of fruit juice. They can be very nutritious. They can be made in ice cube trays.
- Explore grocer's shelves for foods that need no refrigeration such as soup and noodle dishes.
- Keep track of the cost of your snacks. You may be spending more than if you ate at restaurants.
- Avoid sodas since they are very costly and have little food value. You could carry a pack of sugar with you and end up with the same food value at much less cost!
- If you MUST be a grazer and can't seem to eat the fruits and vegetables necessary for a good diet, consider nutritional supplements by using complex vitamin pills. Don't, however, overdose. Eating too many of the fat soluble vitamins (A, D, E, K), which store in your body, can cause you trouble. Read the labels on the vitamin supplements for your body requirements per day.

Cooking with Small Appliances

There are many small appliances available that can make cooking more simple. They do require storage space that is not always available. If you have just one room, small hotplates and other appliances can be a boon to cooking. The important thing to remember is that electricity can be a friend or an enemy. Improperly used, fires can occur. This is especially true in an older type building with limited electrical lines and outlets. Overloading circuits should blow fuses, but overloading is dangerous. So **take safety precautions:**

- Unplug appliances not in use.
- Stay in room when using appliances.
- Surface should not tip and should be heat proof.
- Use only heavy duty extension cords if needed.
- Use only one appliance at a time.
- Read instruction **before** use and follow instructions.

Dorm Room Cooking

There are rules about cooking in dorm rooms. The rules are made for your safety. Microwaves and cooking areas may be available. Some dorms allow small appliances such as irons, hot pots, coffee makers, popcorn poppers, and sandwich makers. **Check carefully to make sure what these rules are and follow them.**

Cooking in a Hot Pot

Hot pots are really just pots with the cooking element inside rather than underneath like a range.

Soups can be made with bouillon cubes, packaged soup mixes, or canned soup. Follow label directions.

- 1 vegetable bouillon cube with a can of tomato soup
- 1 package green pea soup with canned beef bouillon
- 1 can condensed bean and bacon soup, 1 can condensed beef soup, 1 1/2 cans water
- 1 can condensed cream of tomato soup, 1/2 soup can milk or water, 1 can spaghetti
- 1 can condensed cream of chicken soup, 1 can condensed chicken noodle soup, 1 1/2 soup cans of water
- 1 can chicken broth, 1 can water, 1 or 2 eggs stirred into hot soup...Egg drop soup!

Beverages can also be made in the hot pot. Grocers carry teas, coffee, and mixes. Try:

Hot Spiced Cider
- 2 cups cider or plain apple juice
- 2 tablespoons brown sugar or honey
- A pinch of cinnamon, cloves, or allspice

Toddy
- 1 can (12 oz) vegetable cocktail
- 1 can (10 1/2 oz) condensed beef bouillon

South of Border Coffee
- 1 cup coffee
- 1 teaspoon non-dairy creamer
- Dash of cinnamon
- 1 teaspoon sugar

Mocha
- 1 cup water
- 1 teaspoon instant coffee
- 1 packet hot cocoa mix
- 1 marshmallow (if you have one!)

Minted Coffee

    1 cup water

    1 teaspoon non-dairy creamer

    1 tablespoon instant coffee (or as you like it)

    1 piece peppermint candy (crushed)

Stick-to-the-Ribs Foods can be cooked in a hot pot too. Try canned foods of Spanish rice, chicken fricassee, pastas, stews, and chili. Watch so food doesn't stick. Stirring can be helpful.

Hard Cooked Eggs

    Cover eggs with water.

    Bring water to boil. Allow to sit 15 minutes.

Hot Dogs and Beans

    Warm canned pork and beans.

    Add hot dogs whole or in slices.

Chili Dogs

    Warm together 2 hot dogs,

    1 (8 oz) can chili.

    Put on 2 hot dog buns with

    chopped onions.

Hot Dogs

    Cook in water in pot.

STAY SAFE!
Follow Dorm Room Rules!

Emergency Food Supplies

Sometimes unforeseen events temporarily affect our food supply...electrical, snow and ice storms, illness, blocked roads, flooding, or localized power failure can keep you from getting to a store or cooking the food that you have. Keeping some special supplies on hand, especially if you are not in a dorm room situation, can be helpful. Stored foods for real emergencies should:

- Not need refrigeration.
- Be edible without cooking if necessary.
- Be in small enough size so that there are no leftovers to store.
- Not require a large amount of water for preparation.
- Supply appropriate nutrients.
- Be rotated so that they stay fresh and edible.
- Be stored in an area that is dry (cans don't rust), cool, and clean (avoid rodents and insects).

These can be stored in a small area on an emergency shelf, box or basket. (1-3/4 cubic feet of space is estimated for storage sufficient for one person for two weeks.) This space can be in a basement, kitchen cupboard, or closet.

Some suggestions of appropriate emergency foods are:

    Canned chili, spaghetti, and other one dish meals

    Canned an dehydrated soups

    Canned or dried meat

    Ready-to-eat cereals stored in metal containers

    Peanut butter

    Canned fruits, vegetables, puddings

    Flavored drink granules

    Fruit juice concentrates, instant cocoa mix, non-fat dried milk

    Dried fruits and nuts

Sometimes there may not be facilities for cooking. **Carefully consider** any alternative heat source such as fireplaces, camp stoves, outdoor grills, candles, gas appliances if electricity is out, Hibachis, and fondue pots. **Cautions: Fireplaces must be vented. Fuel-burning camp stoves or charcoal burners can give off fumes that are deadly. Candles can cause fires. Take all possible precautions!**

Check in the "Cook 'n Shop" chapter of this book for information of how to keep food safe for eating in case of emergencies.

The Unexpected Guest Emergency

Unexpected guests can be a less urgent emergency. Recipes that you like can be chosen and supplies for these recipes can be kept on hand for just such an emergency. Your choice could be something as simple as spaghetti, canned spaghetti sauce, and dried Parmesan cheese. Quick mixes of all kinds are available.

Cook 'n Shop

"What do I need to know if I want to cook for myself?"

Cooking Helps

If you choose to cook real meals, rather than "grazing" or eating prepared meals at home, you may have to learn "how to." There are many cookbooks that are available for you to use as resources. There is some basic information that may not be available in the normal recipe books such as basic cooking terms, equivalents, substitutions, abbreviations, and measuring instructions. Here are helps.

BASIC COOKING TERMS

Bake: To cook in the oven.

Baste: To brush liquid over food as it cooks.

Beat: To mix fast with an over-and-over motion with a spoon or beater.

Blanch: To dip into boiling water for a short time.

Blend: To mix ingredients until smooth.

Boil: To cook until bubbles rise and break at the surface of liquid.

Braise: To cook covered with small amount of liquid or in steam.

Broil: To cook under direct heat or over coals.

Brown: To cook until the surface of the food is brown.

Chill: To place in cold place, such as refrigerator, to lower the temperature of the food.

Chop: To cut into small pieces.

Coat: To cover food completely, usually with flour.

Combine: To mix ingredients.

Cream: To soften and blend until smooth and light by mixing with electric mixer or spoon.

Cube: To cut food into small pieces with six sides.

Cut in: To mix shortening with flour until finely divided by using two knives or pastry blender.

Deep fat fry: To cook in fat which completely covers the food. This is sometimes called French frying.

Dice: To cut into very small cubes, about the same size.

Dot: To put small pieces of one food on the top of another food, such as butter on a casserole.

Drain: To pour off liquid or allow it to run through the holes of a colander or sieve.

Firmly pack: To press ingredient, such as brown sugar, firmly into measuring cup to make sure the amount is correct.

Fold: To combine by using two motions, one to cut through the mixture, the other to slide across the bottom of the bowl to turn over the mixture. This keeps the air in the mixture.

Freeze: To place in freezer until firm.

Fricassee: To cook by braising. Food is usually cut into pieces.

Fry: To cook in hot fat.

Grate: To rub food over a food grater to break it into small pieces.

Grease: To rub the surface of a utensil with shortening to prevent food from sticking.

Grind: To put food through a food chopper or grinder.

Julienne: To cut into small, thin strips that resemble match sticks.

Knead: To fold and press dough with the heel of hand.

Melt: To heat until a solid becomes liquid.

Mince: To cut into very fine pieces.

Mix: To stir two or more ingredients together.

Pan broil: To cook uncovered in ungreased pan, pouring off fat as it accumulates.

Pan-fry: To cook uncovered in a small amount of fat.

Pare or peel: To cut away outer skin.

Pinch: A very small amount of an ingredient that can be held between finger and thumb.

Poach: To cook gently in hot liquid which is below the boiling point.

Roast: To cook in dry heat, uncovered, usually in oven.

Saute: To cook uncovered in a small amount of fat.

Scald: To heat liquid just below boiling point where bubbles form at edge, or, to pour boiling water over food, or, to dip food into boiling water for short time.

Shred: To cut into thin strips using a shredder.

Shortening: Fats that are either oil or solid such as lard, butter, margarine, and vegetable oils.

Sift: To put dry ingredients through a flour sifter or sieve to aerate and separate.

Simmer: To cook over low heat until liquid forms small bubbles.

Soften: To allow food to sit at room temperature until if gets soft.

Steam: To cook over steam that is rising over boiling water.

Steep: To cover with boiling water and let stand until color and flavor is appropriate (i.e. tea).

Stew: To cook slowly in liquid for a long time.

Stir: To mix slowly with spoon or fork.

Stir fry: To cook in small amount of oil over high heat using a tossing motion.

Toast: To brown by direct heat in toaster or oven.

Whip: To beat very fast with electric beater, wire whisk or rotary beater so that air is incorporated to make ingredients light and fluffy.

COOKING ABBREVIATIONS

Few grains = f.g.	Quart = qt	Square = sq
Teaspoon = tsp or t	Gallon = gal	Hour = hr
Tablespoon = tbsp or T	Ounce = oz	Minute = min
Cup = c	Pound = lb	Inch = in
Pint = pt	Dozen = doz	

EQUIVALENT MEASUREMENTS
Dry and Liquid Measures

3 teaspoons = 1 tablespoon	2/3 cup = 1/2 cup plus 2 2/3 tablespoons
4 tablespoons = 1/4 cup	5/8 cup = 1/2 cup plus 2 tablespoons
8 tablespoons = 1/2 cup	7/8 cup = 3/4 cup plus 2 tablespoons
12 tablespoons = 3/4 cup	

Few grains, dash, or a pinch = less than 1/8 teaspoon

16 tablespoons= 1 cup

Liquid Measures

1 cup = 8 fluid ounces	2 tablespoons = 1 fluid ounce
2 pints = 1 quart	2 cups =16 fluid ounces = 1 pint
4 quarts = 1 gallon	4 cups = 32 fluid ounces = 1 quart

Dry Measures

16 ounces =1 pound

8 quarts = 1 peck

4 pecks = 1 bushel

How to Measure

There are correct ways to ensure quality products by measuring with standard measuring cups and spoons.

Granulated (white) sugar: If it is lumpy, sift it. Then spoon lightly into "dry" measuring cup. Do not tap. Level it off with a straight-edged knife or spatula.

Brown sugar: Remove lumps by rolling or pressing it through a sieve. Pack it into a "dry" measuring cup until sugar holds its shape. Level with a straight-edged knife or spatula.

Confectioners' sugar (powdered sugar): Sift to remove lumps. Spoon lightly into "dry" measuring cup. Do not shake. Level with spatula.

Flour: Sift through sifter or sieve. Spoon lightly into "dry" measuring cup until it overflows. Level with spatula. (When your recipe doesn't specify "sifted flour," spoon flour into "dry" measuring cup to overflowing. Level with spatula.)

Shortening: Pack solid shortening, which is at room temperature, into appropriate size "dry" measuring cup. Level with spatula. Be careful to avoid air pockets. For measurements of less than 1/4 cup, use a tablespoon. Pack shortening into spoon. Level with spatula. For approximate measuring of "stick" shortening, cut according to the marks on the wrapping.

4 sticks (1 lb = 2 c)   1 stick (1/4 lb = 1/2 c)   1/2 stick (1/8 lb = 1/4 c)

Dry ingredients: Stir to break lumps. Using standard measuring spoons, fill appropriate spoon, level off with spatula.

Eggs: When using eggs in recipe that doesn't call for whole eggs, break eggs together. Mix with fork. Pour into "liquid" measuring cup. Look at eye level to see accurate measurement.

2 medium eggs = 1/3 cup	2 large eggs = 1/2 cup
3 medium eggs = 1/2 cup	3 large eggs = 2/3 cup

Liquid: Measure into "liquid" measuring cup placed on level surface. Look at eye level to see correct measurement.

Food Equivalents

1/4 lb cheese	= 1 cup shredded
1 cup whipping cream	= 2 cups whipped
1 lb sifted flour	= 4 cups
1/2 lb pastas	= 4 cups cooked
1 cup rice	= 3 1/2 cups cooked
1 cup precooked rice	= 2 cups cooked

1 lb brown sugar	= 2 1/4 cups, packed
1 lb granulated sugar	= 2 1/4 cups
1 lb confectioners' sugar	= 3 1/2 cups, sifted

Substitutions

If you don't have the ingredients in your cupboard that you need for a recipe, you can substitute with what you may have on hand. These substitutes may not create a perfect recipe, but they should work.

1 regular marshmallow	10 miniature marshmallows
1 T cornstarch	2 T flour
1/2 T flour (used for thickening)	1/2 t cornstarch **or** 1 T quick cooking tapioca
1 c sifted all-purpose flour	Sift 1 c unsifted all-purpose flour. Remove 2 T.
1 c sifted cake flour	7/8 c sifted all-purpose flour **or** 1 c minus 2 T sifted all-purpose flour
1 c all-purpose flour	1 c plus 2 T cake flour
1 c sifted self-rising flour	1 c sifted all-purpose flour plus 1 1/2 t baking powder and 1/2 t salt
1 cup butter	7/8 c vegetable oil, 1 c margarine **or** 7/8 to 1 cup hydrogenated fat plus 1/2 t salt
1 t baking powder	1/4 t baking soda plus 5/8 t cream of tarter
1 oz baking chocolate	3 T cocoa plus 1 T fat (can use oil)
1 fresh glove garlic	1/2 t garlic powder
1 t fresh ginger	1/2 t ground ginger
1 cup white granulated sugar	2 c white corn syrup and reduce liquid in recipe **or** 1 c well-packed brown sugar **or** 3/4 c honey and reduce liquid in recipe
1 c whole milk	1 c reconstituted nonfat dry milk plus 2 1/2 t butter or margarine, or 1/2 c evaporated milk plus 1/2 c water, **or** 1/4 c sifted dry whole milk powder plus 7/8 c water
1 cup buttermilk or sour milk	1 T vinegar or lemon juice plus enough sweet milk to make 1 c; let stand 5 min. **or** 1 3/4 t cream of tartar plus 1 c sweet milk
1 cup sour cream	1 c plain yogurt or 7/8 c sour milk plus 1/3 c butter
1 c buttermilk	1 cup plain yogurt
1 t lemon juice	1/2 t vinegar
1 c light brown sugar	1/2 c dark brown sugar plus 1/2 c granulated sugar
1 c honey	3/4 c sugar plus 1/4 c liquid (use the liquid called for in the recipe)
1 c dark corn syrup	3/4 c light corn syrup and 1/4 c light molasses
1 c light corn syrup	1 c sugar plus 1/4 c liquid (use the liquid called for in the recipe)
12 graham crackers	about 1 c crumbs
1 t baking powder	1/4 t baking soda plus 5/8 t cream of tartar
1 T active dry yeast	1 pkg active dry yeast or 1 cake compressed yeast
1 whole egg	2 egg yolks

Keeping Food Safe to Eat

Getting what is often termed "stomach flu" is most often a food-borne illness. The culprits? Clostridium perfringes. Staphylococcous aureus. Salmonella. Clostridium botulinum. Do these names sound menacing? They are! They reproduce quickly in warm moist places.

WAYS TO PREVENT FOOD-BORNE ILLNESSES

Look and Smell!

1. If a can is bulging, leaking, or foaming, throw it away.

2. If food has an abnormal color, appearance or odor, throw it away. DON'T EVEN TASTE IT!

3. Discoloring on the inside of a can should not be a problem. FDA prohibits use of any food container that will transfer a poisonous or harmful substance to the food in a can.

When Cooking

1. Hot foods should be kept hot at 165-212 degrees F. Cold foods should be kept in refrigerator at 40 degrees F or lower. Freezers should be 0 degrees F or lower. The in-between temperatures are dangerous. **Do not leave hot food out at room temperature for more than two hours.**

2. Cook foods thoroughly, especially poultry.

3. Don't interrupt the cooking process. Cook at one time. As food cools, bacteria develop.

4. Cool foods quickly in small quantities in separate containers so center doesn't stay hot.

5. Marinate food in the refrigerator if it has to stand out for more than one hour.

6. Follow the same precautions if you carry picnic or brown bag lunch food. Place in containers that keep foods cool with or without ice. A sandwich can be frozen in the freezer before packing. It will thaw before you eat it later. (Some foods, such as lettuce and mayonnaise do not freeze well.)

Freezer Safety

1. Date foods put into the freezer.

2. If freezing fresh meats, remove them from original wrap and rewrap in freezer paper.

3. Divide meats into usable portions (i.e. chicken breasts needn't be frozen together). Hamburger can be separated and formed into individual patties for easy use. Separate portions with wax paper.

What to Do If Power Fails

1. If power goes out in your freezer, food will generally stay safe about 2 days if freezer is full. If half full, it will stay frozen about 1 day. Add block ice or dry ice to help hold temperature. (25 lbs of dry ice keeps food frozen for 2 to 3 days if 10-cubic-foot freezer is full or 3 to 4 days if only half full.) Don't handle dry ice with your bare hands! Open door as little as possible.

2. To protect refrigerated foods, put them in the freezer section with extra ice.

3. Do not refreeze raw meats and poultry unless ice crystals are present. Any raw or cooked meat and poultry that remains above 40 degrees for more than 2 hours should be thrown away.

Thaw Safely

1. Thaw meats in the refrigerator, in the microwave, or under cold water in waterproof covering.

2. DO NOT thaw or clean meat on kitchen counters or, especially, on bread boards.

3. Do not thaw commercially frozen stuffed turkey before cooking.

Get Rid of Mold!

1. Moldy foods can be dangerous. If molds are colored, they are ready to produce spores that can produce toxins that harm you. Do not smell moldy food. It can cause respiratory problems.

2. Throw moldy food away. Carefully place it in a plastic or paper bag to keep spores from spreading.

3. Throw away moldy soft fruits and vegetables, breads, peanut butter, nuts, dried grains, and lentils.

4. To remove mold safely from hard cheese and salami, cut off 1" around and below the mold spot. Don't touch the mold with a knife. (Some Italian and "San Francisco" dry salami is covered with a white mold. There should be no other color noticeable.)

5. Hard fruits and vegetables can have mold cut

from the surface the same as hard cheese.

6. Remove a small amount of mold on jellies and jams with a spoon. Take another clean spoon and scoop out around the spot. If it smells fermented then throw it away.

7. Keep your refrigerator clean and sweet smelling by wiping with solution of 1 T baking soda to 1 qt warm water.

Put Groceries Away Quickly

1. When you bring groceries home, put them away immediately.

2. Keep wrapped meat in its wrappings. If wrapping is torn, rewrap. Freezer paper gives protection.

3. Carefully examine packaged foods.

Most Important! Keep Things Clean!

1. WASH YOUR HANDS! (Especially after using the bathroom, sneezing, or nose blowing!)

2. Keep nails clean and don't sneeze over food.

3. Clean food area with hot soapy water after any preparation (especially raw chicken.)

4. Sterilize bread boards with soap and bleach solution. (Use 1 T bleach per 1 quart water.) Clean with clean brush and cloth. DO NOT use steel pads. Small slivers can contaminate food.

5. Wooden bread boards have proven to be safer than plastic ones according to latest studies. Boards can be coated with melted paraffin wax to fill pores of wood to keep them safer.

6. Don't wipe up spills on the kitchen floor with dish cloth.

7. Pet dishes can be contaminated. Don't wash them with the dishes you use unless in a dishwasher that sterilizes. Pet food shouldn't contact other food since it's not prepared under human sanitary conditions.

8. Keep foods covered.

Storing Food Safely

New methods of preservation generally keep your foods safe, but there are things you should know. Refrigeration and freezing do **not** keep bacteria from growing **nor** does it kill bacteria. It merely slows down its growth.

Many foods are dated on their containers to show the consumer when they should be used to have their best flavor, texture, nutritional value, and color. There is no hard and fast rule about when they may be unfit to eat. There are, however, indicators. Foods have bad odors. Mold may form. Cans bulge. Meats become slimy. There are some general rules that have been tested by government agencies that can serve as a guide. These rules are not the final word, but should be tempered with common sense.

FOOD STORAGE TIME AND TEMPERATURE TABLE

FOOD	HOW TO STORE	REFRIGERATOR	FREEZER
CANNED FOODS	In dry, moderately cool areas	Not necessary	No
	Refrigerate if open	Varied	No
BREADS			
Commercial	Room temperature, covered container	Not necessary	3-9 months
	Refrigerator retards mold, doesn't protect freshness		
Home-made	Same as above	Not necessary	3 months
Frozen	Freeze immediately. Wrap	No	1-1/2 months
CEREALS	In airtight containers at 70 degrees	Not necessary	Not necessary
DAIRY PRODUCTS	Check code date to judge length of storage		
Pasteurized milk, cream	Refrigerate quickly in original, closed container	Opened, 1 week	No
Flavored milk	Same as above	Unopened, 20 days	
Sour cream	Same as above	2-3 weeks	No
Butter	Same as above	1-2 weeks	1 year
Soft custards, puddings	Cool quickly. Cover. Refrigerate immediately	3-6 days	No
Hard cheeses	Store tightly wrapped. If mold forms, cut it off.	1 month	3-6 months
Soft cheeses	Store tightly wrapped	2 weeks	Only creamed cheese
Cottage cheese	Cover tightly	10-30 days	4 weeks
EGGS			
Fresh, in shell	Store in original carton, small end down	10 days-5 weeks	No
Fresh, yolk and/or whites	Break out of shell. Blend yolk with white or other whites. Add small amount of salt, sugar, or corn syrup	2-4 days	1 year
Hard cooked in shell	Refrigerator in covered container.	5 days	No
Egg salads	Refrigerate quickly. Keep refrigerated until used	1 day	No
FRUITS			
Ripe fruits	Store in refrigerator fruit/vegetable drawer. Wash before storage, except berries. Can ripen at room temperature.	Varies; watch for mold/decay	Prepare for freezing
Bananas	Store at room temperature	No	Only if for cooking or eating frozen

FOOD	HOW TO STORE	REFRIGERATOR	FREEZER
Fruits with odors	Wrap for storage	Varies; watch for mold/decay.	Prepare for freezing.
Dried	Store in cool, dry place, tightly covered.	Not necessary	No
Frozen	Put in freezer immediately, wrapped.	When unfrozen	8-12 months
VEGETABLES			
Most fresh	Store in refrigerator vegetable drawer. Remove decay, mold, blemishes, and wash. Crisp if needed. by rinsing and wrapping in plastic or covered container.	Varies; watch for mold, decay and sprouts	Prepare for freezing (Not for cabbage, celery, lettuce, or watermelon.)
Tubers and roots (potatoes, onions, turnips)	Store in cool, dry, dark place	Varies; watch for mold, decay and sprouts	Must be prepared for freezing
(carrots, and beans)	Store in refrigerator vegetable drawer	Varies; watch for mold	Must be prepared for freezing.
Frozen	Store in freezer immediately.		8-12 months
Frozen French fries	Store in freezer immediately.		2-6 months
MEATS			
Raw meats	Refrigerate immediately in coldest part. Wipe surface of meat. Wrap loosely. For freezing wrap tightly.	3-5 days	Beef 6-12 months Fresh pork 3-6 months Veal, lamb 6-9 months
Smoked ham, fully cooked	Refrigerate immediately in coldest part. Freezing not recommended.	1 month	1-2 months
Sliced bacon	Refrigerate in original wrapping. Freezing not recommended.	2 weeks	1 month
Processed meats, cold cuts	Wrap in wax paper. Freezing not recommended.	1 week	1-2 months
Cooked meats, gravy	Cool. Refrigerate immediately. Cover tightly.	2-3 days	2-3 months
Frozen meat	Store immediately in original container.	2-3 days	Beef 6-12 months Veal, lamb 6-9 months Pork 3-6 months Sausage/ground 1-3 months Sausage/cooked 1 month
POULTRY			
Fresh, whole, pieces	Rinse cavity with cold water. Wipe dry. Wrap.	2-3 days	9-12 months
Cooked	Cool. Refrigerate in two hours. Cover.	2-3 days	6 months
Poultry salads	Refrigerate after preparation.	1 day	No
Frozen	Refrigerate in original container or cover well.	2 days after defrosting	6 months
FISH			
Fresh	Refrigerate; loose wrap or place in covered container.	1-2 days	1-9 months
Cooked	Refrigerate; loose wrap or place in covered container.	3-4 days	1 month
Frozen	Store in original container.	Use immediately	3-6 months
Smoked	Refrigerate tightly wrapped.	1 week	6 months, Quality deteriorates quickly

If you want further information, call:

Meat and Poultry Hotline
800-535-4555
In Washington, DC area 447-3333

FDA Seafood Hotline
800-332-4010

For other food safety questions, look in the Yellow Pages for: U.S. Food and Drug Administration (Safety of food products not containing meat), Environmental Protection Agency (Pesticides), Cooperative Extension Service (Food handling, nutrition and storage)

Shopping For Food

If you can plan ahead to have any extra money to buy food at lower prices when they are available, you can really save dollars. (This type of shopping requires some storage space.) Before you shop, read newspaper ads to take advantage of "specials." Preplan your meals to allow substitution of sale food. Check cupboards to see if you have everything you need for your meal plans. Plan to go alone when you shop. If you ride with someone, shop alone. You will buy more if you go when you're hungry. Buy only what you need. Shop quickly and go only as often as you must.

Money Savers

Foods To Avoid

Analyze snack foods for food value and cost. Buy snacks high in nutrition. Compare them to the original foods (i.e. fresh potatoes = 20 cents per lb compared to potato chips = $1.50 per lb). Sodas are very expensive for the food value that is in them. Use them sparingly or not at all. A 12 oz soda is equal to three tablespoons of sugar or none at all if you drink diet sodas. If you drink only one per day, the cost over a year can be as much as $150.00 and more if you use soda vending machines. That's a lot of money compared to an equal amount of sugar!

Low Cost Foods

The food portion of your budget is one of the largest parts. It also tends to be cut when money runs low. There are some foods that give you the greatest nutritional value for the least amount of money:

pastas	dried beans and other legumes*
eggs	peanut butter
rice	potatoes
foods that are plentiful, in season	
cabbage	carrots
tuna	corn meal
store specials	hamburger
dried milk	oatmeal

*If flatulence (gassiness) from beans bothers you, soak the beans in water before cooking. Throw the water away and then cook.

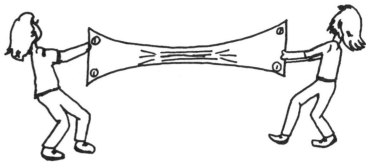

"Loss Leaders" or "Specials"

Foods are sometimes sold under cost and are advertised to get you into the stores to do other shopping. (Read the small print to see expiration dates of sale.) You can take advantage of "loss leaders" by buying ahead for later use or just buying the specials and doing other shopping elsewhere. Some stores lower prices on some foods but raise prices on others. Some sale items are lower priced in other stores. Become aware of prices.

Transportation Costs

When deciding where to shop to take advantage of sales, consider the cost of transportation. If you can't walk, consider shared rides, bus, or bicycle. Shopping at convenience stores can be costly since bread and milk are usually the only foods that are competitive. Planning your shopping in advance and buying at larger grocery stores can save money.

Buying Meat

Meat is the most expensive part of a food budget. Plan your meat purchases to avoid waste and overeating. Eat only requirements suggested by the Food Pyramid Guide.

Description of meat	3 oz Servings per lb
Little or no fat or bones	3 to 4 per lb
Some fat and bones (chicken, round steaks, roasts)	2 to 3 per lb
Much bone (T-bone steaks, ribs)	1 to 2 per lb
Processed meats	
(ham, luncheon meats, frankfurters, sausage)	3 to 4 per lb
Whole chicken	2 per lb
Chicken breasts	2 to 4 per lb

Special Brand Names

Consider house brands, private labels, and generic brands when shopping. They are generally priced lower than nationally advertised brands. Take home one item to try. If you like it, buy more.

Food Ad Help

Read food ads in the newspaper on Thursday and Monday. The Thursday ads are best because all produce is fresh for weekend sales. Compare ads and choose what is low cost for the week.

In Season Foods

When foods are "in season" they are tastier and more reasonable. When the market is full, prices are low. (Just plain old economics!) Storing canned or frozen foods at this time can save money.

Case Lot Sales

Case lot sales can save money if supply is overstocked at beginning or end of the season. Compare prices with regular costs of similar products.

Two For One Sales

Two for one sales may also be good buys. Check prices against the regular costs of similar products.

At the Check-Out Counter

- Check prices of foods as you are checking out. Make sure you have a full view of the cash register and scale. (You can carry a hand calculator with you.) If an error is made or if product is not satisfactory, come back with the receipt. There should be no problems in doing this.
- If you weigh food in the produce section, make sure the scale is set at zero as you start.

Prepackaged foods should also be checked for correct weights.

- If you find that a coupon you are using at the check-out counter is out of date, don't be too embarrassed to return the item. If there is a coupon item you really want and couldn't find, ask for a "raincheck."

Coupon Shopping

Use coupons only if you: really need or want to try the product; normally use the brand or product; buy it at the lowest price compared to similar quality brands; mail in rebate claims (add mailing costs). Check expiration dates. Watch for in-store coupons. Sometimes stores honor competitor's coupons.

Advertising...Don't Believe Everything!

When a store says its prices are the lowest in town, check many of their prices, not just those they advertise. Advertising gimmicks such as selling at low cost or giving items like dishes when you shop require comparisons. Consider the amount you must spend to take advantage of the offer, whether you must buy more than you need, and the cost if you purchased the item elsewhere.

Packaging

Packaging can be costly so you should buy products with the least packaging details. For an example, food in bags is usually less costly than food in boxes. (Also helps with recycling cost!)

Close-out Displays

Close-out displays can be a gimmick to attract the unaware customer. The jumbled display makes a person think these are real bargains. Compare the prices with other products.

"Unit pricing"

Unit pricing is printed on the edge of shelves stating the exact cost of the product per measured unit so you can compare between brands. Sometimes box and can sizes can be deceptive.

Read Labels and Compare

Since labels list ingredients in descending order, whatever is first on the label is what there is most of in the can. (i.e. The first item on the list of ingredients may be water in one can and second on another.)

Read Freshness Codes

Freshness code dates are often put on packages such as bread, processed meat, dairy products, and various boxes. They may be hard to find and hard to read. Choose the latest date for longer lasting use.

Choosing Eggs

Egg prices can be confusing. Use the "Rule of 7" when buying eggs: If the next size (small, medium, large, jumbo, etc.) is 7 cents or less more, buy the next highest size.

> If a can of food is 2 cents less than another on a 20-cent item, the savings is not just "pennies". It's 10% of the price. If you can save that percentage on every item of your yearly food budget, you save a great deal of money!

Choosing Foods

Making food choices can be challenging when trying to get good quality, your money's worth, and the right product for recipes. Not knowing the difference between baking soda and baking powder can produce cookies and cakes like rocks. Trying to choose a ripe pineapple or a fresh fish can be difficult. There are many hints that can save you time and money.

Eggs

Eggs are graded according to freshness and weight. Most eggs available in groceries are Grade A. The freshest quality is Grade AA. The difference is in taste and firmness of the white and the yolk. A fresh egg does not spread out in a pan when broken. The yolk stands high, not flat. Eggs that are not so fresh can be scrambled or used in cooking. If you are not sure if the egg is fresh enough to use, break it into a saucer and look. If it smells bad, throw it away. If an egg has a crack in it, be sure to cook it thoroughly.

The sizes of eggs are:
Jumbo 30 oz/doz
Extra Large 27 oz/doz
Large 24 oz/doz
Medium 20 oz/doz

Small 18 oz/doz
Peewee 15 oz/doz

Fats/Shortenings

Recipes call for shortening or specific types of fats*:

Butter: made from the fat of cream.

Margarine: made of vegetable oils such as corn, cottonseed, soybean that have been partially hardened by hydrogenation process.

Soft margarine: like regular margarine, but has less hydrogenated oils.

Lard: made from fatty tissue of hogs.

Low-fat margarine: varied ingredients; often includes more liquid, less fat.

Vegetable shortenings: made from vegetable oils that have been hydrogenated.

Vegetable oils: made from oils of seed or nuts such as corn, cottonseed, peanut, soybean, olive, safflower, coconut, and oil palm.

*When recipes call for "shortening," butter, vegetable shortenings, or margarine can usually be used. Oil should not be used unless specifically stated. Soft margarine can also be used, but **low fat soft margarines, whipped butter, or water added butters or margarines** can cause problems because of their added liquid content. Butter offers flavor, but acts differently than hard fat in cookies.

*Lard and hydrogenized fats are not as healthy for you since they are saturated. Oils or soft margarines are more healthful.

Flours

Different types of flour are generally made from wheat unless designated differently. The amount of gluten in the flours creates different types of products. You should use enriched white flour for cooking unless otherwise specified.

Enriched flour: has had vitamins and minerals added (most flours are enriched).

Self-rising flour: has had leavening agents and salt added; use this when directed.

White flour: is made from the center of the wheat (endosperm).

Whole-wheat flour: is wheat flour that has different proportions of the natural parts of wheat that are not in white flour.

All-purpose, general-purpose flours: are blends of soft and hard wheat used in most cooking.

Bread flour: is made from a blend of wheat that includes more protein (used mostly by bakers).

Cake flour: is milled from soft wheat that is finely ground; used for fine baked products.

Instant flour: (instantized, instant-blending or quick-mixing flour) is granular all-purpose flour that blends easily with liquid.

Pastry flour: is usually made of soft wheat. This is not quite as fine as cake flour.

Leavening Agents

Leavening agents are air, steam, or a microbiological or chemical agent that can produce carbon dioxide when activated. More simply, they cause foods to rise and become lighter. Examples:

Air: is beaten or folded into mixtures. It expands when heated. (Angel food cake)

Steam: is formed in any batter or dough when it is heated. (Popovers)

Baking soda: when mixed with an acid such as vinegar or sour milk, forms carbon dioxide bubbles. The action is immediate when the acid is mixed with the soda, so add the soda to the dry ingredients. Then add the liquid and mix. Don't delay the baking. (Cake)

Baking powder: liberates some carbon dioxide in the cold batter and then liberates more when the product is baked. (Cake) There are different types of baking powder. The double acting gives the greatest satisfaction.

Yeast: is a microscopic, unicellular plant that produces carbon dioxide when used with sugar, moisture, and temperature. (Breads)

Compressed yeast: is a moist mixture of yeast and starch. Must be refrigerated.

Active dry yeast: is a dry mixture of yeast and starch.

Fruits

There are some general guidelines for choosing fruits of good quality. There may be times, however, that the highest quality is not necessary. For example, apples used for pies or tomatoes used for sauces can be lesser quality. Fruits do lose some nutritional value as they age. Fruits should be firm, unblemished, and well-colored. Decay can usually be spotted at the stem end of the fruit. There are some specific fruits that have special requirements.

Grapes: should be firmly attached to the stem with no discoloration visible. A bleached color around the stem usually indicates that the fruit has been injured or that the quality is poor. They should not be wrinkled or soft.

Citrus fruits (oranges, grapefruit, lemons, etc.): should have firm, unblemished, bright-looking, smooth skins. They should be heavy for their size which indicates they are juicy. Tangerines should have a deep yellow or orange color and bright luster. They will not be firm to the touch.

Cantaloupes (muskmelons): should have the stem completely gone, with a smooth basin where the stem was. The netting should stand out from the surface. The color between the netting should be a yellowish color. There will be a pleasant cantaloupe odor and the stem end will yield slightly when pressed with a thumb.

Watermelon: is difficult to judge if not cut open. A whole melon should have a relatively smooth surface that is neither shiny nor dull. Ends should be rounded and filled out. There should be a creamy color on the underside. If you buy a cut melon, choose one with good red color, free from white streaks. Seeds should be dark brown or black.

Berries: should appear clean with a uniform good color appropriate to the berry. They should be firm, not mushy. There should not be stem caps present. (If strawberry caps are still on, they should be bright green, not dried). Look at the bottom of containers to see if there is staining present. This usually indicates poor quality, overripe berries.

Pineapples: have a fragrance when ripe. The color should be golden yellow, orange yellow, or reddish brown. The pips should have a slight separation. They flatten when ripe.

Milk

Milk generally refers to cow's milk. There are other varieties such as goat's milk in some localities.

Whole milk: has at least 3.25 percent milk fat (butterfat).

Pasteurized milk: has been treated by heat to kill harmful bacteria.

Homogenized milk: has been pasteurized and been treated to reduce the size of fat globules so that the milk doesn't separate from the cream.

Vitamin D milk: is milk to which Vitamin D has been added.

Fortified or multivitamin milk: has had vitamins A, D, niacin, thiamine, riboflavin, and minerals such as iodine added.

Skim milk: is milk that has less than 0.5 percent butterfat.

Low-fat milk: has a range from 0.5-2 percent butterfat.

Acidophilus milk: (nonfermented) has added lactobacillus acidophilus culture added to low fat milk for persons who have milk allergies.

Chocolate milk: is milk that has had sugar and chocolate added to it.

Chocolate drink: is made from varied ingredients. There is less butterfat in it. There is also, generally, less milk.

Buttermilk: is milk that is left when fat is removed from milk, or sweet or sour cream during the churning process. It contains at least 8.25 percent milk solids other than fat.

Yogurt: has a bacterial culture added to whole or partly skimmed milk. Sometimes flavorings and/or fruit are added.

Evaporated milk: is whole cow's milk from which 60 percent of the water has been removed. Skim milk is also available.

Sweetened condensed milk: has had half of the water removed from whole milk and has added sugar of about 44 percent.

Dry milk: has had the water removed from the milk.

Non-fat dry milk: has had the water and fat removed from the milk.

Wash 'n Wear & Care 'n Repair

"How do I take care of my clothes?"

Laundry

When it's time to do the laundry, there are choices to make. You can:

- Send dirty clothes home for the family to clean for you. (Will they?)
- Take clothes to the local laundromat and do them yourself. (Can you get there?)
- Take clothes home to wash them. (Do you live close enough or have enough clothes to last between trips?)
- Send them to a professional laundry. (It's costly.)
- Wash the clothes where you live using available equipment. (Are washers and dryers there?)
- Get a friend to do them for you. (That's a REAL friend!)
- Wear them dirty. (Will you have any friends left?)
- Throw them away and buy new ones. (Now that can be fun, but costly!)

When making a choice, consider the cost, time involved, imposition on others, washing facilities available, and your personal knowledge.

Six Basic Steps for Doing Laundry

Many people feel that washing clothes simply means throwing the clothes into the washing machine with some detergent and then throwing them into the dryer to dry. If you follow that process, you may turn clothes a different color, shrink woolens, and cover clothes with lint. Clothes may rip, tangle, or wrinkle. Spots can appear from stains not treated.

Because washing clothes can be costly and time consuming, and you may not have enough clothes to form separate loads, you may choose to make some compromises. The following information can be handy to have as a guide and reference even if you've been doing your own laundry for a long time.

> If you choose to use a coin operated laundry, you might like to create a laundry tote to carry your supplies. Collect change and place in the tote. Be sure chosen laundromat is clean, well lit and maintained.

STEP #1 Read the Labels and Analyze Fabric if Necessary

Because there are so many different kinds of fabrics that require individual care, the government has created a Care Labeling of Textile Wearing Apparel Law. It requires that most garments have care labels permanently attached on an overwrap on packaged garments, or on securely attached hang tags. Labels must also be on draperies, sheets, bedspreads, tablecloths, suede and leather wearing apparel, towels, upholstered furniture, and slipcovers. These labels give information on fiber content and care instructions in a brief form. Explanations of some of the less obvious terms may be helpful.

LABEL INSTRUCTION HELPS*

MACHINE WASH	Wash, bleach, dry and press by any customary method. Can commercially launder or dry-clean.
HOME LAUNDER ONLY	Same as machine wash, but don't launder commercially.
NO CHLORINE BLEACH	Use only oxygen bleach.
NO SPIN	Remove wash load before final spin cycle.
DELICATE CYCLE GENTLE CYCLE	Wash by hand or use delicate, gentle machine cycle.
DURABLE PRESS CYCLE PERMANENT PRESS CYCLE	Use permanent press cycle or warm wash, cold rinse, and short spin cycle.
WASH SEPARATELY	Wash alone or with similar colors.
HAND WASH	Launder by hand in lukewarm water. Can dry-clean or bleach.
HAND WASH ONLY	Launder by hand in lukewarm water. Can bleach. Do not dry-clean.
HAND WASH SEPARATELY	Launder by hand with similar colors or alone.
DAMP WIPE	Clean surface with damp cloth or sponge.
TUMBLE DRY	Dry in tumble dryer at specified setting.
TUMBLE DRY REMOVE PROMPTLY	Remove immediately when tumbling stops. if no cool-down cycle is used.
DRIP DRY	Hang wet. Hand shape and allow to dry.
LINE DRY	Hang damp. Allow to dry.
NO WRING	Hand dry, drip dry, or dry flat only.
NO TWIST	Handle carefully to prevent wrinkles and distortion.
DRY FLAT	Lay garment on flat surface to dry.
BLOCK TO DRY	Maintain original size and shape while drying.
IRON DAMP	Dampen fabric before ironing.
DRY-CLEAN ONLY	Dry-clean only using professional or self-service.
PROFESSIONALLY DRY-CLEAN ONLY	Do not use self-service dry-cleaning.

* Based on the Voluntary Guide of the Textile Industry Advisory Committee for Consumer Interest. The American Apparel Manufacturers Association, Inc. Rev. 1972.

INTERNATIONAL SYMBOLS ON CARE LABELS

 • Tells safe water temperature for washing the garment.

 • It is safe to use bleach.

 • Can dry the garment in the dryer.

 • Varied numbers of dots tells how to press: one dot means a cool setting; two dots means a medium setting; three dots means a hot setting.

 • It is safe to dry-clean the garment.

 • X through a symbol means not to use the method!

What If the Label Isn't There?

If a label is missing and you don't know what the fiber used is, you can do a simple "burn test." Use a small ball of fuzz that you pull from a sweater or a small piece of fabric cut from an inconspicuous spot of the garment, such as a facing. Place the piece on a dish that will not melt or be hurt by heat. Touch a burning match to the fiber. Look at what's left and analyze the results.

- Wool forms an ash and smells like hair burning.
- Cotton, linen, and silk leave a gray ash.
- Synthetics melt into a small, hard ball.

If the only information on a label is the percentage of fibers, care for it as you would the fiber with the highest content. Then use the following information to figure how to launder specific fabrics.

Understanding Fibers and Their Care

Synthetic or man-made fibers: include 21 generic names with over 200 trade names such as Dacron, Nylon, Acetate, and Spandex. The fibers are similar to plastic straws. They will melt when hot, bend when warm and retain shape in which they cool. They do not absorb liquids easily. For these reasons, use cool to warm temperatures for water and for iron; dry at moderate heat; remove from dryer while still warm to prevent wrinkling.

Natural fibers: include cotton, ramie, silk, linen, and wool.

Wool, which is made from sheep hair, must be treated gently or it will lose its sheen and size.

Silk, made from silkworm cocoons, is very fragile and needs gentle handling.

Cotton, ramie, and linen, made from plants, can usually tolerate more heat and abrasion.

MAJOR SYNTHETIC (MAN-MADE) FIBER INFORMATION

Fiber	Uses	Laundering comments
Acetate, Triacetate	Linings, sleepwear, draperies, quilted jackets & comforters	-Do not use chlorine bleach. -Do not rub, wring, or twist. -Do not soak. -Use only warm temperature in water, dryer, iron. -Use fabric softener.
Acrylic, Modacrylic	Sweaters, knit garments, sportswear, sleepwear, socks, blankets, pile fabrics.	-Use low heat for water, iron, and dryer. -Avoid rubbing and twisting if fabric "pills" (forms small balls on surface). Turn garment inside out. -Use fabric softener. -Use chlorine bleach only if first tested.
Anidex	Sportswear that stretches, lingerie, hosiery	-Use only warm water and steam iron or warm iron. -Can tumble dry, warm temperature.
Nylon	Dresses, blouses, hosiery, slacks, sweaters, jackets, purses, sportswear	-Use warm water, dryer, and iron. (Hot water OK if heavily soiled and white or colorfast.) Cold water minimizes wrinkles. -Use fabric softener to avoid static electricity. -Wash white nylon separately to avoid permanent color transfer. -Can use chlorine bleach, but test first.
Polyester	All types of apparel, often combined with other fibers	-Wash same as nylon. -Pretreat, especially for oily stains.
Rayon	Dresses, blouses, shirts, pants, jackets, linings, draperies	-Use gentle agitation. Hand washing is preferred. -Some rayons require dry-cleaning. Check label. -Use warm temperatures in water, dryer, and iron. -Press on wrong side with moderately hot iron.
Spandex	Swimwear, ski pants, foundation garments, often blended with nylon	-Machine wash using warm temperature for water, dryer, and iron. -Non-chlorine bleach preferred.

NATURAL FIBERS INFORMATION

Fiber	Uses	Laundering comments
Cotton	Apparel, diapers, household fabrics such as towels, sheets (Cottons are often blended with other fibers like polyester.)	-Machine wash. Can use hot water, dryer and iron on whites and colorfast items. -Can use chlorine bleach on white and colorfast items. (If there's no label, use non-chlorine bleach.) -See note above for fabric blends. -Dampen evenly before ironing using sprinkling or spray bottle. Keep garment items covered and allow moisture to spread for at least two hours. -Steam pressing usually doesn't remove wrinkles unless blended with synthetic fibers.
Linen	Dresses, suits, shirts, tablecloths, towels	-Same as cotton but can use very hot iron. -Do not press in sharp creases.
Ramie	Sweaters, blouses, trousers, sportswear	-Same as cotton -Often used with a blend of other fibers. -Follow label instructions.
Silk	Apparel, scarves	-Follow label instructions. Often need dry-cleaning. -Use gentle action, warm water, dryer and iron. -Do not soak. Dyes may fade. Wash separately. -Do not use chlorine bleach.
Wool	Apparel, socks, blankets (See special problems for washing sweaters.)	-Same as silk. Check label for washability. -Use special wool soap such as Woolite in cool water. -Some garments need blocking to original shape. Dry flat. -If wool is untreated, agitate only one or two minutes for washing and one minute for rinsing. -Hand washing is preferred on small garments.

Fabric blends, such as polyester/cotton, should be treated as the weaker of the fibers, in this case, polyester. Remember that synthetics do not withstand heat and chlorine bleach well.

STEP #2 Sort

1. Sort Items by Color and Fabric

White & colorfast cotton garments & linens

Separate white clothes from deep colors. Can be washed in warm or hot water. Can also use cold water with cold water soap.

Light colors

Separate and wash in warm or cold water.

Dark colors

Separate and wash in warm or cold water.

Fluorescent colors

Wash separately in water temperature appropriate for fabric.

Hand-painted, tie-dyed, blocked prints

Avoid fading by "setting" colors. Place in water and vinegar solution before washing. Turn inside out. Wash according to type of fabric.

Machine washable wools

Use cool water and short wash cycle.

Permanent press, synthetic

Separate according to fabric treatment. Read label.

Terry cloth and lint creators like fuzzy rugs, sweatshirts

Place articles together since lint will transfer.

Throw rugs

Wash separately.

Hand washables, loosely-knit, lacy items

Don't wash with towels. Read label. Use gentle cycle or wash by hand.

2. Sort Items by Amount of Soil

Greasy, very dirty

Wash separately. Can presoak. Use extra soap or detergent.

If you have very small loads when you sort, consider carefully before doing ALL of the clothes together. NEVER put deep colored, non-colorfast clothes with lighter color clothes unless you don't care about items changing color. Clothes that need gentle handling or create fuzz should be separated. Heavily dirty, oily pieces can transfer the dirt onto other clothes too. If you do choose to wash some of the clothes together, ignoring the risks, use cold water and cold water soap. This will offer some protection. Don't forget to turn jeans inside out!

STEP #3 Prepare Each Piece

- Place delicate garments in mesh bag or pillowcase.
- Turn inside out: permanent press garments with permanent creases or prints, knits, blue jeans.
- Close hooks and zippers. Knot drawstrings to avoid their pulling out.
- Empty pockets. (Tissues and pens make a terrible mess!)
- Brush lint out of cuffs and pockets.
- Loosely knot all belts, strings, and long stockings to prevent tangling.
- Repair holes or tears so they won't rip more.
- Remove any trims that may fade.
- Treat stains, spots, and heavy soil.

STEP #4 Remove Stains

Heavy Stains or Soil

If clothes are heavily soiled or stained, soak in laundry detergent or pre-soak product completely dissolved in warm, not hot, water for 30 minutes. Pre-soak detergents with enzymes work well on protein based stains such as milk, eggs, grass, chocolate, blood, urine, baby formula, and certain complex stains. Sort fabrics. Follow label directions. Wring out, spin out, or press out soak water before washing in clean water.

Most Small Stains and Soil Lines

There are various ways to remove stains and soil lines. Use the special treatments suggested in stain removal charts for difficult stains. Spray, stick, or liquid pretreatment stain removers can be used following directions on container.

General Rules for All Stains

- Check label before beginning.
- Remove stains as quickly as possible. If unsure of origin of stain, wash in cool or warm water. If stain is on garment requiring dry-cleaning, get it cleaned as quickly as possible. Let clerk know origin of stain and type of fabric.
- **Test stain remover on a part of the garment that can't be seen (i.e. a seam or a facing). Touch the area with a drop of the stain remover and leave it for 2-5 minutes to see if the fabric is adversely affected.**
- Always follow directions on any laundry product.
- All stains may not come out. Heating with water, dryer, or iron can "set" stains.
- Work in a well lit area on a clean surface that is protected from harm.
- Place stained area of fabric toward a paper towel or clean white towel. Wipe on the back of the stain to force it out rather than through the fabric. Use only a few drops of the remover at a time, making sure not to add it faster than it is being absorbed.
- If there is a mark left after using the removal process, treat the whole garment with the pretreatment stain remover and rewash. If you were using a bleaching product, the whole garment must be bleached. Color may change but will be uniform.
- Launder the garment after using remover to wash out stain and remover.
- All fluorescent colors should be tested for color-fastness before cleaning.
- Velvet made of acetate fibers mats down. Don't use water or water based spot removers.
- Never use cleaning fluids or solvents on leather or suede.

DANGER!!!

- Store stain removers safely where they can't be reached by children.

- **Do not mix products!** Mixtures of ammonia and chlorine bleach or liquid detergent and chlorine bleach mixed full strength make deadly fumes. If two different stain remover products are used, rinse one out well before using another.
- Don't breathe solvent fumes such as carbon tetrachloride. Work in well ventilated area. Don't get chemicals near your face.
- Wash up any chemical spills immediately from surface. Protect surfaces as you work.
- Chlorine bleach is not safe for all fabrics. Read label.

SUPPLIES THAT CAN BE USED FOR STAIN REMOVAL:

•Alcohol	Rubbing alcohol or denatured alcohol (70 to 90% concentration) with no color or perfumes.
•Ammonia	Use household ammonia with no color or perfumes.
•Amyl Acetate or Finger Nail Polish Remover	Chemically pure amyl acetate (banana oil) is sold at drug stores. Use finger nail polish remover with no oil. If remover with oil is used, follow with dry-cleaning solvent.
•Bar Soap	(Example: Fels Naptha)
•Chlorine Bleach	Liquid bleach is available in grocery stores.
•Color Remover	This is sold with dyes. (Example: Rit)
•Combination Solvents (Boosters)	Product sprayed on or rubbed in to remove stains. Contain solvents to remove oil and water based stains. (Example: Spray 'n Wash, Stain Stick)
•Detergent	Use liquid hand dish-washing detergent. Other detergents may set stains.
•Dry-cleaning Solvent	Dry-cleaning solvents are available in many stores. (i.e. Energine or Carbona) Don't buy product containing hazardous perchlorethylene.
•Dry Spotter	This is prepared by mixing: 1 t mineral oil and 8 t dry-cleaning solvent.
•Enzyme Product (Digestant)	These come as presoak or enzyme-containing laundry detergents. Mix with water just as it is ready to be used so strength isn't lost. (Examples: Biz and Axion)
•Glycerine	This is available at drug stores.
•Hydrogen Peroxide	Use a 3% solution sold as a mild antiseptic. Sold in drug stores.
•Oxygen Bleach	This dry bleach is safe for most fabrics. Available in boxes in grocery stores. Test first!
•Wet Spotter	Mix 1 T glycerine, 1 T liquid hand dish-washing detergent and 1/2 c water. Shake well before using.
•White Vinegar	Some colors change when using vinegar. If this happens, rinse well with water and add a few drops of ammonia to color changed area. Rinse well with water.

Note: Since there are so many different types of dyes, fabrics, and stain ingredients, there is no guarantee that the stain removals suggested will work. It is best to test on hidden area if possible.

STAIN REMOVAL CHART
FOR WASHABLE FABRICS

TYPE OF STAIN	PROCESS
Adhesive, gum, rubber cement	Rub with ice; scrape off with dull knife; sponge with dry-cleaning solvent; rinse; launder.
Beer	Blot with dry cloth. Rinse with solution of cool water and vinegar. Rinse. Apply digestant. Bleach with appropriate bleach if necessary.
Beverages: (Coffee, tea, soft drinks, fruit juices, mixed drinks)	(Follow each step until stain disappears. Then wash.) 1. Soak for 15 minutes in solution of 1/2 t liquid dish-washing detergent and 1 T vinegar in 1 qt warm water. Rinse with warm water. 2. Sponge with alcohol. Wash. 3. Soak for 30 minutes in solution of 1 qt warm water and 1 T enzyme product. Wash. 4. If stain still remains, dab with chlorine bleach (1 t bleach to 1 T water). (Use chlorine bleach only on white or colorfast cotton fabrics. Some polyesters and blends are safe...test first.) Leave bleach on only for 2 minutes or less. Wash.
Blood	Rinse with cold water or let soak. Use enzyme product if available. Wash as usual. Can bleach if fabric is white or colorfast.
Candle wax or Crayon	Remove surface wax with dull knife. Place stain between paper towels and press with warm iron. Change paper often. Dab remaining stain with dry-cleaning solvent. Dry. Launder. If necessary, use safe bleach. (Can call 1-800-CRAYOLA)
Chalk	Brush with soft brush; wash with laundry detergent. If stain remains, use safe bleach.
Chocolate	Use a combination solvent. Launder. If stain remains, treat stain directly with enzyme presoak or detergent. Launder.
Coffee	Soak with enzyme presoak or oxygen bleach; rub in detergent; wash in warm to hot water.
Cosmetics	Dampen stain; rub with detergent; sponge with dry-cleaning solvent; rinse; launder in hot water if safe for fabric.
Egg	Scrape with dull knife; soak in cool water with enzyme presoak; rub in detergent; launder.
Feces or Stool	See urine. If necessary, use safe bleach.
Fingernail Polish	Sponge with non-oily fingernail polish remover (or amyl acetate) on back of stain. Change paper as needed. Repeat until stain is gone. Launder. Use mild bleach if necessary.
Fruit and Fruit Juices	See beverages.
Grass	Soak in enzyme presoak rinse; rub with detergent; wash in water as hot as fabric tolerates; if stain remains, sponge with alcohol. Wash.
Gravy	Scrape with dull knife; soak in enzyme presoak. Rub on liquid detergent or granular detergent paste, then treat with dry-cleaning solvent. Launder with safe bleach.
Grease	Heavy-duty liquid laundry detergent, a paste of detergent granules and water, or a bar of laundry soap works best on heavy oil or grease stains. For sturdy fabrics, like jeans, a small washboard works well.
Ice Cream	Soak in enzyme presoak or use combination solvent. Rinse. Rub with detergent. Rinse. Dry. If stain remains, rub with dry-cleaning solvent. Rinse. Launder with safe bleach if necessary.
Ink (Ballpoint)	Place stain face down on paper towels. Sponge back of stain with dry-cleaning solvent. If any ink remains, rub it with bar soap. Rinse and launder.
Ink (Regular)	Dampen with water. Rub with bar soap. Rinse. Soak in enzyme presoak or oxygen bleach using water as hot as is safe. Launder. If stain remains, use chlorine bleach if safe. Some inks may need a color remover (test first and follow directions). Some inks can't be removed.
Lipstick	Moisten with combination solvent or glycerine. Launder. Bleach with safe bleach.
Mayonnaise	Rub with detergent. Rinse. Let dry. Sponge with cleaning fluid. Rinse. Launder with hot water if safe.
Margarine	See oil or grease.
Mildew	Gently brush off mildew if excessive. (Do it outdoors!) Launder with chlorine bleach if safe for fabric.
Milk	Soak in enzyme presoak. Rub in detergent. Launder.
Mucus	See urine.
Mud	Brush off as much as possible. Soak in water with dish-washing detergent and 1 T vinegar. Rinse. Sponge with alcohol. Rinse. Soak in enzyme presoak. Launder with safe bleach.
Mustard	Pretreat with liquid detergent with enzymes or spray type stain remover. Rinse. Launder in safe bleach and water as hot as safe.
Oil	Apply combination solvent. Launder. Dry. Oil solvent can be used if needed.
Paint (Water Based)	If paint is still wet, rinse in cool water to flush out paint. Apply liquid soap. Rinse. Repeat as needed. Launder. Dried paint may not come out.
Paint (Oil Based)	Pretreat by sponging with solvent recommended on paint container. Use mineral spirits, turpentine, or paint thinner if container isn't available. Rinse. Launder. Dried paint may not come out.
Perspiration	Dampen stain and rub with bar soap. Presoak with enzyme detergent. Launder in hot water with chlorine bleach if safe for fabric. If color of fabric has changed, apply ammonia to fresh stain or vinegar to old stain. Rinse. Launder.
Rust	Apply paste of salt/vinegar. Leave for 30 minutes. Launder. Then use paste of salt/lemon juice. Rinse. Launder. (Can try commercial rust stain remover following directions on container.) (Do not use chlorine bleach.)
Scorch	**(Scorch may not come out since fibers may be weakened. Further damage may occur.)** Can try to soak for 30-60 minutes with enzyme presoak or wet with hydrogen peroxide and a drop of ammonia. Rinse. Wash in water as hot as safe. Rub with suds. Bleach. Dry in sunlight.
Soft drinks	Dampen with cool water and rubbing alcohol or enzyme presoak. Soak in safe bleach using water as hot as safe for fabric. Launder. See Beverages.

TYPE OF STAIN	PROCESS
Tar	Scrape excess with dull knife. Place face down on paper or fabric towel. Sponge back of stain with tar remover, mineral spirits, prewash spray, turpentine, or dry-cleaning solvent. Change towels frequently. Launder in water as hot as safe for fabric.
Tomato or Tomato Product	Sponge with cold water. Use combination solvent. Rinse. Rub with detergent. Use vinegar or a digestant. Launder in water as hot as safe for fabric using safe bleach.
Urine	Presoak in ammonia solution of 1/4 c to 1 gal of water for five minutes. Then treat with mixture of vinegar and water. Rinse. Use digestant if needed. Launder with safe bleach in water as hot as safe for fabric.
Vomit	See Urine
Wine	For fresh stains, saturate with club soda. Launder. Or saturate with mixture of dish-washing liquid and vinegar. Launder.

STEP #5 Wash

- Load washer making sure items can move freely in water. **Don't** overload. To avoid tangles, **don't** wind large items around agitator.
- Add laundry detergent or soap of your choice. Follow package directions. Can add water softener to hard water. Use slightly less detergent or soap if water is softened, if the load is small, if items are only lightly soiled, or if using small amount of water.
- Choose appropriate water temperature and washing action. (Cold water is excellent for rinsing.)
- Set the control dials on the machine according to the type of items you will be washing.
  Normal loads use regular cycle with warm to hot temperature settings depending on amount of soil.
  If wash 'n wear cycle is needed and there's none on machine, wash in cold water rinse to cut down on wrinkling during the final spinning process.
- Remove items from machine immediately when finished to avoid wrinkles.

LAUNDRY PRODUCT INFORMATION

Soap	Traditional cleaning substance. Water softener is recommended to avoid scum if water is hard.
All-Purpose Detergent	Powder or liquid detergent suitable for laundry and other household cleaning. Referred to as heavy-duty detergent. Can be high or low sudsing.
Laundry Detergent	Special detergent that cleans many different fabrics. Some are effective at lower washing temperatures; others soften fabrics, control static and wrinkles.
Light Duty Detergent	Created for lightly soiled, delicate garments when heavy cleaning's not required.
Wool Cleaners	Cleaners specifically designed to clean wool (i.e. Woolite.)
Chlorine Bleach	This chemical cleans, whitens, brightens and removes stains, disinfects, and deodorizes. Recommended only for white and colorfast cotton fabrics.
Oxygen or All-Purpose Bleach	This chemical produces more gentle bleaching action than chlorine bleach. Recommended for fabrics that should not use chlorine bleach.
Enzymes and Enzyme Presoaks	This washing product breaks down certain soils and stains. Should not be used in combination with chlorine because it deactivates the cleaning action.
Bluing	Blue coloring added to wash or rinse water. Counteracts yellowing of white fabrics.
Starch	Supplies body and stiffness to garments. Can be sprayed on while ironing. Dry starch can be mixed according to directions on package, then fabrics can be dipped into it. Sprinkling and ironing are required to create smooth surface.
Water Softener	An agent that inactivates or removes water hardness minerals.

STEP #6 Dry & Iron (If Appropriate)

Automatic clothes dryer drying

- Use appropriate setting for the items.
- Be sure to empty the lint filter before starting the dryer.
- Don't overdry fabrics especially underwear and socks. Allow elastic bands to remain slightly damp when removing from the dryer. (Delicate lingerie lasts longer if air-dried.)

I WONDER IF IT WILL ALL FIT?

- Don't dry natural and synthetic fabrics together. They need different drying times and temperatures.
- Remove from dryer immediately to avoid wrinkles, especially if you do not have a cool down cycle.
- Turn garments right-side-out and hang on hangers. Fold other clothes appropriately for storage.
- If dryer doesn't have a permanent press setting, allow about 25 minutes drying time and remove items immediately. Place on hangers for cooling and complete drying.

Line drying

- Hang on line or over special clothes dryer to dry. When hanging on lines, place clothespins to avoid wrinkles. Windy days fluff fabrics. Ironing may be needed.
- When hanging clothes, straighten them as much as you can to cut ironing time.
- Be sure clothespins and line are clean.

Ironing

- Read instructions in instruction booklet that comes with iron.
- Set iron dial for appropriate fabric. There are usually four settings:
  1. Synthetics—lowest temperature for man-made fibers.
  2. Wool—medium temperature for wool, silk, and blends of cotton and synthetics.
  3. Cotton—for 100% cotton or when ironing with a pressing cloth.
  4. Linen—highest temperature for pre-dampened, untreated 100% linen. (Pretreated linen uses setting between cotton and linen.)
- If steam pressing, follow instructions for filling iron. Unplug when filling with water.
- Follow the grain of the fabric when ironing. Look carefully at the fabric to see in which direction the threads are running. Press in the same direction to avoid wrinkles.
- Hang on hanger or fold appropriately when finished.
- Do not iron puffish, hand painted or silk screen designs. This causes prints to crack.

SPECIAL IRONING HELPS

Shirts or Blouses

Press in the following order:
  1. Press seams open on inside of garment (unless they appear to go in one direction or are sewn shut.) Press on inside of garment to remove wrinkles and moisture from seams.
  2. Press facings (These are the linings at the edge of areas such as collars and lapels that often show on the outside of garments.)
  3. Press insides of pocket flaps and cuffs, areas around buttons. (Don't scratch iron on buttons.)
  4. Then press in order: trims such as bows and ruffles, collar and cuffs, sleeves, yoke (ironing from sleeve to sleeve), body of garment.

Trousers or Slacks

Press in the following order:
  1. Press inside of waistband, zipper facing, and pockets. (Do not press hot iron over nylon zipper.)
  2. Put top of pants over end of ironing board and press outside from top of waistband to bottom crotch.
  3. Place one part of pants lengthwise on the ironing board, putting leg seams of one pant leg together. Steam iron inside of pant leg from crotch to bottom hem.
  4. Turn over and press inside of other leg in same way.
  5. Place two legs together, lengthwise on board. Steam press each outside of legs from waist to hem.

FOLDING FITTED SHEETS

  1. Tuck all four corners of sheet into each other.
  2. Lay out flat on surface. Fold sides that form.
  3. Complete the folding into size you prefer. Smooth the sheet as you fold it.

SPECIAL LAUNDERING PROBLEM

Laundering by Hand

- Use solution of 1/8 to 1/4 c granular all-purpose detergent or one long squirt of light-duty liquid detergent for one gallon of warm or cool water.

Swish water to mix granules if used.

- Do just a few items at a time. Squeeze water through items causing others to wash against each other. Do not scrub hard or twist. Rinse thoroughly in cool water.

Wool Sweaters

Dry-cleaning is recommended unless wool is designated as washable. Most sweaters, however, can be washed if done as follows:

- Use only cool water with special cold water cleansers such as Woolite.
- Hand wash unless label says it can be machine washed. Do not twist, rub, or stretch when wet. Gently squeeze solution through the fibers. Rinse well and press water out with hands. Do not wring. Finish water removal by rolling in towel.
- Lay flat on a waterproof surface to dry. Stretch sweater into desired shape. (Make an outline of sweater on paper that will not fade or transfer color. Stretch or mold the sweater into the correct size.)

Silk Garments

- Dry-clean, if recommended.
- If washable, launder gently in lukewarm water with detergent compatible with silk. Rinse in lukewarm or cold water. Dry on gentle cycle or hang to dry. (Remove excess water by rolling in towel.) Never wring water out.
- Iron on reverse side at low temperature. May need to iron while damp. Washable silks can be ironed with steam iron on low temperature.

Down-Filled Items

Follow care label instructions. If there are no instructions, but you still want to wash the item:

- Add laundry detergent to water first and fill machine half full. Submerge item. Finish filling washer. Balance wash load with towels or similarly colored other down-filled items.
- Use regular agitation and normal spin. If necessary, stop washing action to remove air from items.
- Wash sleeping bags separately.
- Dry, using low temperature. Add dry towels and

a clean pair of tennis shoes to fluff the down filling.

Electric Blankets

Follow the care label instructions. If not available, consider washing using gentle agitation and normal spin in warm water. After removing cord, protect plug on blanket by folding and carefully pinning to corner of blanket. Air dry by spreading over two bars or clothesline.

Care of Clothing

Keeping clothes in good repair saves resources, especially dollars. Taking care of what you have allows you to have money for other things. Taking care of clothing also tells people about your organizational skills and what you value.

SHOE CARE

- Protect shoes from weather. Polish leather shoes to preserve them for longer wear and comfort.
- Prepare new leather shoes by using a water repellent polish or spray. Then polish with shoe polish.
- Fabric and vinyls benefit from waterproof sprays.
- If shoes get wet, stuff lightly with crumpled newspaper and dry at room tempcrature. Apply shoe cream or saddle soap to soften leather. When dry, polish with shoe polish.
- If shoes are marked with salt stains, remove the stains as soon as possible with a desalter product or sponge carefully with water. Then clean with saddle soap to soften leather. When dry, use shoe polish.
- Soft grained leather should have stains removed quickly using mild soapsuds solution. Dry. Polish.
- Clean suede and napped leather with a bristle brush or art gum eraser. An emery board or fine sandpaper roughs up nap. These shoes can be ruined by wet weather.
- Clean synthetic shoe materials with detergent solutions. Lighter fluid, carefully used, can remove tar or asphalt marks. Sometimes toothpaste can remove marks.

- Simulated straw and fabric materials need special cleaners. Remove light soil with detergent and water solution. Cleaning solutions remove stubborn grease stains.
- Patent leather usually cleans with a damp cloth. Special polish is available to clean and recondition.

Other Shoe Hints

- To avoid rot, consider not wearing shoes or boots two days in a row, especially if your feet perspire a lot.
- Compare prices for repairing shoes. Repair may not be worth the price. If you do repair, get a receipt for a claim check. When done, try them on to see if they still fit.

STORING CLOTHES

Avoid extra ironing, dry cleaning, and deterioration from moisture and insects with thoughtful storage.

Repair First

- Repair clothing right away so it can be used.
- Repair garments before washing or dry-cleaning to avoid further damage.
- If needed, brush clothes or use lint roller before putting them away so they are ready to wear.
- Fabrics that "pill" can be shaved with a special shaver or brushed with stiff-bristle brush.
- Remove any stains promptly. If necessary, take item to the cleaners as soon as you can.

HELPS FOR CLOTHING REPAIR

Simple clothing repairs can be done without the aid of a sewing machine. There are, however, hand held machines that can do seam repair quickly and effectively. The simple **back stitch** is the strongest stitch of all. This hand stitch is used to mend seams and also areas that need to be reinforced:

A **catch stitch** is used to sew hems on stretchy fabrics.

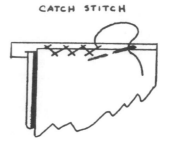

CATCH STITCH

Overcasting stitch is used to sew on patches, appliques and fasteners. It is also used to finish raw edges of seams or hems.

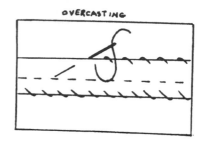

OVERCASTING

Backstitching is used for mending open seams or fastening two pieces of fabric together.

BACK STITCHING

Hemming or slip stitching is used when you don't want the seam to show on the outside of a garment, such as for hems.

1. Fold the fabric over 1/4 inch and press, or sew with running stitches. Hemming tape can also be sewn on.
2. Turn the fabric to the correct place for hemming and press.
3. Stitch so the stitches are not visible on the outside.

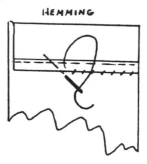

HEMMING

When **sewing buttons,** a shank can be made to give strength to the button and allow room for fabric when buttoned.

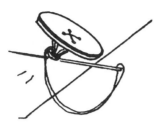

When **sewing buttons on a coat front,** a smaller button is used on the inside for extra strength.

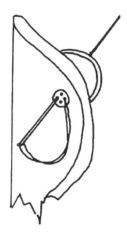

How to Hang Clothes for Storage

- Be sure that clothes are dried completely before storage.
- Use wooden, plastic, or coated hangers. Wire hangers can rust on garments in a moist climate.
- Simple "snap" clothespins on wire hangers can hold pants and skirts and avoid hanger lines.
- Take belts off garments so that belt loops aren't strained.
- Be sure that the lapels, pocket flaps, and collars are straight when garments are hung.
- Zip zippers and button one button when hanging clothes to avoid wrinkles and keep shape.
- Hang pants upside down with hem held between two sides of pants hanger.
- Avoid filling a closet too full. Clothes will wrinkle if forced together.

- Fold knitted sweaters and garments rather than hanging them. Be sure the folds do not create wrinkles.
- Closets should be kept dry in moist climates. Special light bulbs or charcoal will be helpful.
- You can add extra insurance by spraying appropriate insecticide around the floor quarter-round at the base of closets where insects hide. Read directions carefully. Keep floors and corners dust free.

How to Prepare for Long Term Storage

- Garments should be protected for seasonal storage to avoid moths, silverfish, and carpet beetles.
- Remove any spots. (Spots get harder to remove the longer you wait.) Dry-clean when appropriate.
- Wash man-made fabrics and even fabrics with moth-resistant finishes so stains don't attract insects.
- Brush garments carefully including cuffs and under lapels and collars.
- Woolens take special care:
  a. Spray woolens with moth proofing spray, following directions carefully.
  b. Place garments in tightly closed container that has moth balls, flakes or crystals, or in a cedar chest or cedar closet. Clean container or closet carefully to get rid of moth larvae. The larvae do the damage, not the moths themselves.
  c. Moth blocks discourage moth entry, but do not remove larvae that are present.

Getting Cleaned Up For Company

"How much do I want to clean and how do I do it?"

How clean do you want your living space to be? Do you want to be able to pass a "white glove" military inspection? Do you want to avoid cleaning at all costs? Do you want to clean only when relatives and friends come to visit? Do you want to be somewhere in-between?

There are advantages to consider for reasonable cleanliness. "Clean" keeps you healthy and discourages bacteria, bugs, and vermin. It protects your investment in things you own so they are usable and resalable. It can make you feel good about yourself. It even protects your security deposit.

Make a Plan That Works For You

If cleaning is something that you really hate, consider sharing the tasks. If you are living with someone, make lists to share. Number tasks according to your individual dislikes and likes, allow for time spent doing the task, and then share them equally by number. Another way to share is to invite someone to join you in big cleaning tasks and return the favor for them. You could have a cleaning party. You could even set up a cooperative with friends so all benefit from sharing the cleaning jobs.

If you choose to work alone, make a game of it. Turn yourself into a time and motion expert and figure ways to do jobs faster. You can also turn on the music...work to the beat!

Clean as you go so there isn't so much to clean at one time. Put things away when done with them!

A chart can help you get started. Set your own schedule to make things only as clean as you want. The "Suggested Timing" offers a plan to keep things clean most of the time. If used, the work won't get ahead of you so that it takes more time later.

MY OWN PLAN

Area	Suggested Timing*	Daily	Weekly	Sometime	Target Date
KITCHEN					
Empty garbage	Daily				
Wash dishes, clean sink and counters	Daily				
Sweep or damp-mop floor	Daily				
Wipe range including reflector bowls	Daily				
Dispose of leftovers	Weekly				
Wipe fingerprints from phone and wall switches	Weekly				
Clean range oven and hood/fan	As needed				
Wipe/polish small appliances	After use				
Wash walls	As needed				
Clean/defrost refrigerator	As needed				
Clean inside of drawers & cupboards	As needed				
Wash windows & curtains	Seasonally				
Clean/strip/wax floor	Seasonally				
BATHROOM					
Wipe sink & counter top	Daily				
Clean walls of shower	Weekly				
Empty wastebasket	Weekly				
Clean toilet	Weekly				
Wet-mop floor	Weekly				
Replace dirty towels	Weekly				
Clean sink, tub	As needed				
Clean mirrors/accessories	As needed				
Clean shower curtain/door	As needed				
Straighten and wipe drawers and shelves	As needed				
Clean windows/curtains	Seasonally				
Clean/strip/wax floor	Seasonally				
RUGS/CARPETS					
Remove spills	Immediately				
Vacuum rugs	Weekly				
Spot clean heavy traffic areas	As needed				
Vacuum under furniture	As needed				
Clean and/or shampoo	Seasonally				
FLOORS					
Sweep or mop	Daily				
Clean and polish	As needed				
FURNITURE					
Dust	Weekly				
Polish	As needed				
Vacuum upholstery	As needed				
Clean upholstery	As needed				
WALLS					
Remove smudges on switch plates, door handles	Weekly				

Area	Suggested Timing*	Daily	Weekly	Sometime	Target Date
Dust to remove dust and cobwebs	As needed				
Clean as appropriate	As needed				
Dust woodwork and doors	As needed				
Wash woodwork and doors	Seasonally				
WINDOWS					
Wipe sills	Weekly				
Wash	As needed				
Wash or dry-clean curtains and drapes	As needed				
ACCESSORIES					
Dust lamps/shades	Weekly				
Clean telephone	Weekly				
Clean media equipment	Weekly				
Wash vases/ceramics	As needed				
Polish mirrors	As needed				
Dust picture frames	As needed				
Polish brass	As needed				
Clean light fixtures	As needed				
BEDROOM					
Air beds briefly before making them	Daily				
Put clothes away	Daily				
Change bed linens	Weekly				
Vacuum/dust	Weekly				
Turn mattress	Bi-monthly				
Move furniture to vacuum	As needed				
Organize closets	As needed				
Wash mattress covers, pads	As needed				
Air pillows, comforters	As needed				
Wash walls, woodwork, windows	As needed				
Wash or dry-clean blankets, spreads	Seasonally				
LIVING ROOM					
Dispose of ashes, papers, clutter	Daily				
Straighten pillows, throws, and accessories	Daily				
Vacuum rugs and upholstered furniture	Weekly				
Dust or vacuum floors, baseboards, doors, corners	Weekly				
Dust and clean accessories/ light fixtures	Weekly				
Empty wastebaskets	Weekly				
Shampoo rugs/furniture	As needed				
Wipe cool lamp bulbs	As needed				
Clean under furniture	As needed				
Wash windows, curtains	As needed				
Clean/wax floors	As needed				
Dust books/pictures	As needed				
Wash walls and woodwork	As needed				
Clean closets	Seasonally				

Know How To Clean

KITCHENS

(Also refer to floors, woodwork, windows, insects, etc.)

Plastic Laminates (i.e. countertops)

- Wipe with detergent solution on dampened cloth or sponge.
- For stains, sprinkle bleach cleanser on dampened surface. Allow to sit for three minutes, then gently rinse. If necessary, repeat process. Do not rub unless absolutely necessary since abrasives scratch.
- Do not use rust removers, metal and oven cleaners, hair dyes and rinses. Wipe spills immediately.
- Never use knives, sharp instruments, or hammer objects on surface.

Ceramics (i.e. tile, kitchenware)

- Remove film and spots with diluted or full strength all-purpose household cleaners (can use solution of 1 part vinegar and 4 parts water). Rinse. Buff. Do not use abrasives that scratch.
- Wash grout with full strength household cleaner, cleanser, or tile grout cleaner. Can clean with a toothbrush in grout areas. For mildew or stain, use solution of 3/4 c chlorine bleach and 1 gal water. Rinse well.

Sinks

- For stainless steel, wash with solution of detergent or all-purpose cleaner and water. Rub in same direction as grain of steel. If using special cleaners, follow package instructions. Rinse. Dry. Steel wool pads can remove stains or discoloration, but cause scratches. Remove water spots with rubbing alcohol.
- For porcelain, sprinkle cleanser on wet surface. Let stand for a minute. Rinse. Repeat if necessary.

APPLIANCES

Refrigerators, freezers, range, automatic dishwasher, dryer, washer

- Recognize material in appliance and choose appropriate cleaning product. Follow directions.
- Clean outside often with sponge or soft cloth dampened with detergent solution. Can rinse if necessary. Wipe.

Ranges

- Wipe spills immediately with paper towel or dry cloth. Watch for hot areas to avoid burns.
- Using hot detergent solution, wash pans under burners and their supports as needed, when range is cool. Rinse. Dry. If pans are made of aluminum, use nylon scrubber or steel soap pad. Wipe metal or porcelain ring around electric surface units. Remove electrical unit when possible and wipe around it. Clean holes in burner ports with small wire or pipe cleaner.
- For thorough cleaning remove gas range burner heads or entire burners. Wash in hot detergent solution, scouring if necessary. Rinse. Dry. If range allows, lift range top and clean underneath with warm detergent solution. Rinse. Dry. Clean oven with oven cleaner following directions. (Or place bowl of household ammonia in oven overnight with the door closed. Wipe with ammonia/detergent solution. Remove stubborn stains with plastic scourer or steel wool.) Clean racks and removable panels in sink with warm detergent/ammonia solution. (Don't mix ammonia and chlorine bleach cleanser.) Rinse. Dry.

> The oven sensor temperature tube on the roof of gas oven or back of electric oven must be wiped gently without bumping or jarring or it may not work! Do not leave cleaning product on tube.

Microwave Ovens

- Wipe interior and exterior after each use, or as needed, with mild detergent and water solution.

- Open oven door when cleaning touch control panel. Wipe panel with cloth lightly dampened with water only. Don't scrub or use any chemical cleaner on control panel. Dry with soft cloth.
- Use mild cleanser with no abrasives to clean soil inside oven. Rinse with damp cloth or sponge. Dry.
- Wipe spills on turntables immediately. Clean under turntable too.
- Check instruction book.

Self-Defrosting Refrigerators

- Get rid of leftover and spoiling food items at least once a week.
- Wipe up spills immediately to avoid stains and bacterial growth.
- Wash, rinse, and dry shelves and storage drawers. Then wash inside walls with solution of 1 T baking soda to 1 qt water. Clean gasket on door with solution of water, baking soda, and detergent.
- Use brush or vacuum cleaner attachment to clean fins and area below refrigerator. Remove and wash evaporator pan that collects water. Also clean condenser coils or fins if they are on back of refrigerator.

Refrigerators That Are Not Self-Defrosting

- Defrost refrigerator when frost is about 1/2 inch thick on freezer compartment. Follow directions in instruction book. If there is no book, turn refrigerator off using temperature control knob. Remove freezer trays and food. Wrap frozen foods in layers of newspaper or place in insulated container.
- To hurry process, place hot water in pans in freezer and/or on shelves. Never chip ice off!
- Empty collected water. Wipe freezer, drawers, shelves, and sides with damp cloth or sponge dipped in solution of soda and water. (See above.) Rinse. Dry. Replace dried trays, drawers, and food.
- If there is a drain hole from freezer to the lower refrigerator, clean by flushing with clean warm water.

- To avoid odors, place open package or dish of baking soda on a shelf. Charcoal also works.
- Turn refrigerator back on.

Small Appliances

- Disconnect before cleaning.
- If cooking appliance is not immersible, wash inside with detergent solution and rinse. If immersible, wash with detergent solution. Rinse. Don't get electric connections wet.
- Clean outside after each use with damp, detergent solution. Rinse. Dry. Polish.
- Do not clean with abrasive scouring pads or use cleaners. Check directions.
- Clean cords by pulling through a damp cloth. (Don't get the plug and cord wet inside.) Dry.
- **Toaster** crumb tray located under toaster needs cleaning. Unplug first.
- **Electric coffee makers** use special cleaners. Follow directions. Wipe outside too.
- **Can opener** wheel should be cleaned with small brush. Run paper towel through process to dry.

BATHROOMS

(Also refer to floors, walls, windows, kitchens)

> **SUGGESTED CLEANING SOLUTION**
> Mix a germicidal or disinfectant liquid cleaner according to directions. Place in a spray bottle to use for general cleaning of kitchen and bathroom fixtures.

Tile Showers (Ceramic or Plastic)

- Wipe surface with a towel or squeegee after each use to avoid build-up of minerals or molds.
- To clean, wipe with cleaning solution, all-purpose household cleaner, spray-type bathroom cleaner, or vinegar/water solution. (1 c vinegar to 4 c water.) Include shower track and track rollers. Rinse. Dry. Clean hair from drain.
- For mold, use commercial product following directions or mix 1 c chlorine bleach to 1 gal water. Soak stubborn stains with soaked paper towels. Leave 15-30 minutes. Rinse well.

- For grout stains, use old toothbrush. (It's best to seal grout for easier cleaning.)

Fiberglass Showers

- Wipe down shower with towel or squeegee after each use.
- Clean with mild disinfectant cleaner and white nylon scrubber pad. Do not use abrasive cleaners, scouring pads, bleach, or harsh acids. Clean hair from drain. Rinse well. Dry.

Bathtubs and Sinks

- Wipe down regularly after each use. Wipe chrome fixtures. Rinse. Dry.
- Clean with disinfectant cleaner, cleanser, spray-type or liquid cleaner regularly. Rinse. Dry.
- If very dirty, sprinkle damp surface with cleanser. Allow to sit for a minute or two. Rinse. Dry. If necessary, repeat cleanser process, rubbing if absolutely necessary.
- For rust or mineral deposits, use foam cleaner. Allow to stand on the surface for up to one minute before wiping it away. Use a brush or nylon pad. A commercial rust remover may remove rust. (Follow directions on container.)
- For quick clean-up, wet tissue and wipe hair from areas and drains. Clean drain stoppers monthly.

Toilets

- Clean with disinfectant using toilet bowl brush. Be sure to wipe under rim of stool. Flush to rinse.
- Wipe upper surfaces and around base of toilet. (Don't forget the handle!)

Counter Tops

- For a quick wipe, dampen tissue or toilet paper and remove surface dirt and hair.
- See Plastic Laminates in "Kitchen" section.

RUGS/CARPETS

> Don't carry dirt in the house in the first place! Ridges on the bottom of shoes hide dirt, stones, and tar. Sand acts like sandpaper on floors and cuts fibers in rugs. Use a synthetic grass type or vinyl/rubber backed nylon mat in front of all doors and wipe feet well.

Carpets

- Vacuum twice a week. (Stroke backward and forward seven or more strokes at least once a week to remove dirt in well traveled areas.)
- Vacuum heavily trafficked stairs frequently working from top to bottom.
- Avoid pulling carpet fringe with an upright vacuum by lowering the vacuum handle as you cross the carpet.
- Sprinkle smelly carpet with plain baking soda. Leave for one hour. Vacuum.
- To avoid static electricity, mist carpet lightly with 1 part liquid fabric softener and 5 parts water. Then dry.
- Remove stains promptly! The longer the stains remain, the more difficult they are to remove.

Removing Carpet Stains

When suggesting how to remove stains in carpets, there is no perfect answer. The chemistry of fibers and dyes used in rugs and the stain ingredients vary. The following suggestions are generally effective, but **not guaranteed**. A professional rug cleaner may need to be called and even they may not be able to remove all stains.

> Test all stain removers in a spot not easily seen such as a corner of a closet.

Stain Remover Solutions

- Detergent solution of 1 t mild liquid dishwashing detergent (no lanolin, non-bleach) 1 pt warm water.
- Detergent/vinegar solution of 1 t detergent, 1 t white vinegar, 1 qt water.
- Vinegar solution of 1 pt water and 1 pt white vinegar.
- Nail polish remover without lanolin base. (Not for acetate or acrylic fibers)

- Dry cleaning fluid of any brand non-flammable spot remover liquid (Read directions).
- Carpet cleaner or shampoo of any brand (Read directions.) (Also see note below on cleaner choice.)
- White soda water. (i.e. club soda, tonic, or 7-Up).
- Paint remover such as turpentine, paint thinner.
- Ammonia solution of 1 part ammonia to 10 parts water. (Never mix with chlorine bleach!)
- Alcohol: rubbing, isopropyl, or denatured. (Denatured is preferred, but is flammable and poisonous.)
- Hydrogen Peroxide—3 to 5% solution.
- There are also commercial spot removers. Use them according to directions on container.

General Instructions

> Remove stain as quickly as possible!

*Special Note: Many newer carpets have special stain resistant finishes. These protective coatings do not allow stain removers to enter fibers. There are often instructions available and a telephone number to call for stain problems. If you're not sure if there is a coating, try a stain removal process of your choice. If it doesn't work, mix 1 T baking soda and 1/4 c water. Rub into spot. Blot. Then use stain remover on it again until there is no trace of stain on cloth. Rinse. Blot. Dry. If you know there is a protective coating over it such as Scotch Guard, remove the coating by adding a squirt of liquid detergent on a damp cloth, rubbing it in, and blotting it up. Then use any stain removal process you choose.

- Remove spilled solids with a rounded spoon or spatula. Then blot as much of the stain as you can before you try to remove it. Use white fabric or white paper toweling. **DO NOT RUB.**
- Choose a stain remover and test it in a spot that won't be seen. Leave on 10 minutes. Blot with clean, white absorbent material and look for color. If remover is safe, continue suggested process until no stain shows on blotting cloth.
- Work from outside edge toward center of stain to avoid spreading.
- **Do not overwet!** Blot frequently.
- Rinse area where stain has been removed to avoid leaving residue that attracts dirt.
- When there is no color left on blotting cloth, cover area with pad of white fabric or paper towels. Put heavy weight on top. (You can stand on it for a minute or so.) Remove pad when dry. Pile may need to be brushed up gently. Vacuum.

STAIN REMOVER SUGGESTIONS

Alcoholic Beverages	Blot. Dilute with club soda, or baking soda and water. Blot. Rinse well. Blot dry.
Blood	Blot. Wet with minimum cool water. Soak and blot until no stain is seen on blotter. Apply small amount of detergent solution. Blot. Apply cool ammonia solution (on synthetics only). Blot. Repeat until stain is not visible on blotting cloth. Rinse. Blot dry.
Candle Wax	When wax is dry, scrape off excess. Use small amount of dry-cleaning solvent. Repeat until stain is not visible on blotting cloth. Blot. or Place brown paper bag over wax. Press with warm, not hot, iron. Keep moving bag to use a fresh spot on the stain until all wax has been absorbed. Use dry-cleaning solvent if necessary. Blot to dry.
Catsup/Tomato Sauce	Scrape off and blot. Apply cool detergent solution. Blot. Repeat as necessary. Rinse. Blot. If stain remains, apply 3-5% hydrogen peroxide solution. Rinse. Blot dry. (Be sure to test before using hydrogen peroxide since hydrogen peroxide bleaches.)
Chewing Gum	Place ice cubes in plastic bag over spot to harden gum. Break up brittle gum. Vacuum up pieces. Apply dry-cleaning solvent to remove residue. Blot. Repeat until no stain is present. Blot dry.
Chocolate	Scrape off or blot. Wet stain with small amounts of rubbing alcohol or dry-cleaning solvent. Blot dry immediately. Repeat until no stain is seen. Wet area with minimum of water. Apply detergent solution. Blot. Repeat until no stain shows on cloth. Rinse with clear water. Blot.
Cigarette Burns	If burn is slight, rub with steel wool or brush lightly. Clip off small charred parts. Shampoo. Dry. If burn is severe, contact professional to replace with "plug" of matching carpet.
Coffee or Tea	Blot. Wet stain with 7-Up or tonic water. Wet and blot until no stain is present. Rinse with clear water. Apply detergent solution. Blot and repeat until no color is present. Rinse with clear water. Blot dry. or Blot. Apply detergent/vinegar solution. Blot. Rinse. Blot dry. Then try dry-cleaning solvent. Blot dry.
Crayon	Scrape off excess crayon. Apply dry-cleaning solvent. Blot. Apply detergent solution. Rinse. Blot dry. (Call 1-800-CRAYOLA.)
Fruit Stains	Blot. Dampen with water. Dump salt on stain. Rub in lightly. After salt sits a few minutes, rub it into the stain. Brush salt out. Vacuum. Repeat until stain is gone. (See instructions for wine if the stain is grape or cranberry.)
Furniture polish	Blot carefully. Apply dry-cleaning solvent. Blot. Apply detergent solution. Blot. Rinse. Blot. Repeat as necessary. Remove stain immediately. This stain is very difficult to remove.
General Dirt	Make a very sudsy solution of a liquid laundry detergent and water. Brush only the suds onto the spot. Brush in horizontal then vertical movements. Blot up excess moisture. Place white toweling over spots and put weights over toweling to help absorb moisture. Rinse with small amount of water by blotting gently. Repeat blotting. Brush up pile gently. Allow to dry completely.
Ink or marker	Blot carefully. Put alcohol, paint thinner, or dry-cleaning fluid on a clean cloth. Blot gently until the spot is removed. Be sure to change the section of the cloth that you use frequently so that the stain is not redeposited on carpet. Let dry. Repeat process if necessary.
Lipstick	Blot if necessary. Apply dry-cleaning fluid. Blot. Apply detergent solution. Blot. Apply ammonia solution. Blot. Apply vinegar solution. Blot. Rinse. Blot.
Milk/cream/ice cream	Blot. Apply ammonia solution. Blot. Rinse. Blot. Apply detergent solution. Blot. Rinse. Blot.
Mud	Allow mud to dry. Vacuum up excess dirt. If spot is left, rub on some denatured alcohol. Blot. Then rub on detergent/vinegar solution. Blot. Rinse. Blot. Brush up pile gently. Dry completely.
Nail Polish	Wipe up excess gently. Apply dry-cleaning fluid on white cloth. (**If carpet is not acetate** you can also use acetone or nail polish remover.) Change area of cloth you are using often so that you do not redeposit the polish. Blot. Apply detergent solution. Blot. Repeat process as long as necessary. Rinse. Dry.
Oil Based Paint	Use paint thinner, paint solvent, or dry-cleaning solvent. Remove remaining stain by softening the paint stain with white towel dampened with paint thinner or dry-cleaning solvent. Allow to remain for several hours. Apply warm detergent solution. Blot well. Apply ammonia solution. Blot. Rinse with warm water. Blot. Dry. May need a professional.
Urine	Urine stains may remove dye from carpet. Treat quickly. Blot up as much as possible. Pour on club soda. Blot again until almost dry. Flush with small amount of water. Blot. Dry. or Blot up excess. Apply detergent solution. Apply ammonia solution. Blot. Apply vinegar solution. Blot. Rinse. Blot. Dry.
Vomit	Carefully remove vomit trying not to force it into rug. Blot carefully. Apply detergent solution. Blot. Apply ammonia solution. Blot. Apply vinegar solution. Blot. Flush with small amount of water. Blot. Dry.
Water Based Paint	Apply detergent solution. Blot. Apply ammonia solution. Blot. Apply small amount of water to rinse. Blot. If stain remains, **test rug** with lacquer thinner in inconspicuous area. If rug doesn't melt, apply to stain to soften dried paint. Then blot. Rinse. Blot. Dry.
Wine Stains	Blot. Wet stain with SMALL amount of 7-Up or tonic water. Blot and repeat as necessary. Apply small amount of detergent solution. Blot. Repeat as necessary. Rinse with clear water. Blot. Dry.

Deep Cleaning Carpets

Rug cleaning can be done professionally. If this is your choice, get recommendations from friends and check with the Better Business Bureau. Be prepared to explain stains to the rug cleaner.

If you choose to do it yourself:

- Try rug cleaner choice where it won't be seen to see if rug shrinks, changes color, or pills.
- Remove furniture or put aluminum foil or plastic under furniture legs. Remove when rug is dry.
- Don't get carpet too wet or it can shrink or stretch. Dry as quickly as possible. A fan or air conditioner is helpful.
- Try out rug cleaning product to see if a sticky residue will remain by putting some in a bowl. Allow it dry. If sticky residue is left, the product will attract dirt. There are various cleaners available:

  - **Dry rug cleaners** come in powdered form or foam to put on and vacuum. Follow directions.
  - **Spray-on aerosol or concentrated rug detergent** can be used with a sponge mop, hand brush, or other applicator. (It's easier to rent a machine than to do it by hand.)
  - **Steam cleaning or water extraction** uses a machine and cleaning solution. Read directions on machine and cleaner. Machines are rented in hardware or grocery stores. Test before using.

FLOORS

Asphalt

Vacuum or damp-mop regularly with 1/2 cup fabric softener to half pail of water using minimum water. Use all-purpose cleaner if needed. Strong solvent cleaners, abrasives, turpentine or naphtha pit floors. Strip and rewax annually using water-based wax.

Brick

Vacuum and damp-mop regularly. If floor becomes dull, use solution of 1/2 c vinegar, 2 T furniture polish, 1 gal water. Seal brick floors to avoid staining. Sealed floors should be stripped, resealed, and waxed with water-based wax annually.

Ceramic Tile—Glazed

Vacuum and damp-mop regularly. (If dull, use vinegar treatment of 1/2 c vinegar, 2 T furniture polish, and 1 gal water.) Use all-purpose, non-abrasive cleaner when needed. For stubborn spots, use liquid cleanser and soft plastic scrubber. For tough stains on grout, apply household bleach and leave for a few minutes. (Dark colored grout discolors from bleach.) Rinse well.

Ceramic Tile—Unglazed

Vacuum and/or dry-mop regularly. Use all-purpose, non-abrasive cleaner when needed. Do not use abrasives, acids, or strong soaps.

Concrete/Cement

Sweep and hose where appropriate. Damp-mop and vacuum where appropriate. When deeper cleaning is required, wet surface first. Then wash with an all-purpose household cleaner according to directions on container. Rinse well. Seal surfaces for easier cleaning. Be sure to clean well first. There are special cleaners that will etch the floor, allowing the seal to be more effective.

Specific problems:

- **Mold** can be removed with 4 parts water and 1 part bleach. Put on with a sponge mop. After a full day, rinse completely using a stiff broom. Wipe dry.
- **Oil** can be removed with kitty litter, sand, sawdust, granulated detergent, or special absorbent. Sweep up well after leaving it overnight. Wash with all-purpose cleaner. Rinse.
- **Rust** may be removed by sprinkling with portland cement. Sprinkle with water and rub in with stiff broom or brush. Rinse.

Linoleum

Vacuum or damp-mop regularly. Use any type cleaner except strong detergents or abrasives. Use minimum water. Wax with water-base or solvent base wax as needed.

Marble

Vacuum and damp-mop regularly with clean water. Floor should be sealed well. If really dirty, wet with clean water and then use appropriate cleaner, following container directions. Rinse well so crystals can't form and destroy floor. Strip, reseal, apply water-based or solvent-based wax annually. Don't use harsh abrasives, since marble stains and scratches easily. Avoid harsh acids. Do not allow acids to contact the surface.

Rubber Tile

Vacuum and damp-mop regularly. Use all-purpose cleaner if needed. To avoid a dull surface, add 1 cup fabric softener to half pail of water for damp-mopping. Do not use paste wax or solvent-based liquid wax. Rewax with water-based wax when needed. Strong sunlight and strong cleaners can damage tile.

Terrazzo

Vacuum and damp-mop regularly using only clear water and mild detergent. RINSE WELL. Avoid harsh abrasives, acids, ammonia or borax. Surface should be sealed well. Strip, reseal, and apply water-based wax or solvent-based paste wax annually. **Test in hidden area.**

Vinyl

Vacuum surface dirt as often as possible. Damp-mop once a week using very little water. Wash and rinse. If floor is dull use a one-step cleaner/shiner or mixture of 1/2 c vinegar, 2 T furniture polish, and 1 gal water. If floor is really dull or yellowed, strip off wax with commercial stripper or a mixture of 1/4 c Spic and Span, 1 c ammonia, and 1/2 gal of water. Clean 3-foot square at one time. Leave solution on for 5 minutes except for tiles. (Soak only 2-3 minutes to avoid loosening tiles. Resoak if necessary.) Rinse well. Rewax following label directions on chosen product. Solvent-base floor wax masks the true color of the floor. Always test first!

Vinyl No-Wax

Vacuum or dry-mop regularly, especially through traffic areas. Use all-purpose cleaner if needed. If floor is dull, apply a gloss-renewing product. No-wax surfaces need wax too (see vinyl floors above.) If floor is dingy (probably from poor rinsing), use recommeded cleaner and water. Wax may need stripping. If floor is sticky, wash with 1/4 c Murphy's Oil soap and 1 gal water. Rinse well. If tiles are yellowing, follow instructions for vinyl surface above. Solvent-base floor wax masks the true color of the floor. Always test your choices first! Follow directions on chosen product.

Wood

Clean floors with furniture-oil-treated mop or vacuum. Spray-mop 12 hours before using so oil penetrates fibers. Find if floor has a surface finish, such as polyurethane or penetrating sealer that is waxed, by rubbing finger across surface. If surface doesn't smudge, it's a surface finish.

Surface Sealed Finishes

Vacuum or damp-mop with misted mop (use water or dust spray) at least weekly. Avoid water. For dirty floors, add 1/4 c vinegar to 1 c warm water. Dip the mop, and ring out until almost dry. Do not wax.

Penetrating Sealed Finishes

Clean at least weekly with dust-treated mop. For grimy floor, wipe with very lightly dampened mop or cloth. If something spills, wipe it up quickly and buff. Wax yearly following directions on container of wax product chosen. (Solvent-based wax preferred.)

FURNITURE

Wood

Dust with soft treated cloth following direction of the grain of the wood. Use polish only when necessary. A water-damp cloth can remove fingerprints. Then buff well.

Care depends upon finish. Test cleaners and polishes in hidden area. Don't switch between polish types. For high gloss finish, use non-oil or paste wax. For dull luster, use cream type wax. Do not wax natural oil finishes. (Rub with boiled linseed oil.) Some spray furniture waxes dust, clean, and polish. Shake container. Spray on surface. Wipe dry immediately. Thoroughly cover very dirty furniture with polish. Clean a section at a time using circular washing motion. Wipe immediately with clean, dry cloth. Reapply polish using label directions. Buff.

For water stain marks, wait 24 hours to see if mark disappears. Then use a half and half olive oil and vinegar solution. Shine with clean, dry, soft cloth. Cover scratches with scratch cover polish, brown crayon, eyebrow pencil, cigar ashes, or rub with walnut half for dark furniture or pecan half for light furniture. Try to match the furniture color.

Wood-like Furniture

Wipe with cloth dampened with water/all-purpose cleaner solution. Rinse. Buff. Never use abrasives or cleaners.

Upholstered Furniture

Vacuum regularly including arms, backs, and under cushions. Remove spots immediately. Clean as you would carpeting of similar fabric. Pretest in hidden area. Do not saturate. Use foam only.

Chrome Furniture

Wash with detergent solution or club soda. Rinse. Dry. Or rub with smooth, damp aluminum foil, shiny side out.

CEILINGS

Generally only bathroom or kitchen ceilings get dirty enough to require extensive cleaning. Refinishing, such as repainting, may require washing beforehand so that the coating will not peel off.

Painted Ceilings

To remove cobwebs or dust, use vacuum attachment or cloth wrapped on head of a broom. Wipe with dry sponge if needed. If washing is necessary, test on least visible area since paint may come off. If repainting is needed, use strong cleaner like TSP or, if less dirty, an all-purpose cleaner. Follow label instructions. Cover floor and furniture with drop cloths. (Plastic will do.) Wear a hat and goggles. Rinse as you work so areas don't dry. Overlap strokes to avoid streaking.

Tiled/Textured Ceilings

- **Vinyl-coated acoustical tile** can be scrubbed.
- **Non-washable acoustical tile** should be wiped with a dry sponge. To remove stains from coated or non-washable acoustical tile, spray with half bleach and half water mixture. Test an area first. **(Protect things with a drop cloth and don't breathe the chemical.)** The best method is repainting. (This limits the acoustical value.) If painting over a stain, shellac stain first so it won't bleed through. You can spray paint.
- **Textured ceilings** can have texture removed by scraping with a board. Then repaint.
- **Textured ceilings** with acoustical finish can be resprayed.
- **Decorative plaster** can only be vacuumed. If it is too dirty, it must be repainted.

WALLS

If walls need cleaning or painting, start at the top and work down. If you are **washing** walls, start from the bottom and work up. Be careful of drips since they mark the wall before you get to them.

Brick Walls

Brush and vacuum when needed. Can use dry sponge if more cleaning seems necessary. If hard, non-porous brick and mortar still need cleaning, use diluted ammonia solution and scrub brush.

Painted Walls

Check the process in an area that isn't noticeable before you make yourself a "big spot." Generally, most walls need only spot cleaning. A quick wipe with a damp cloth may be enough. If the spot is difficult, scour with baking soda and water. Then try a liquid abrasive. If you have a matching paint, just paint over the area if needed.

If area is dirty or you need to wash before painting, check in hidden area to see if paint is washable. Wash from bottom up with a general household cleaner following instructions. Rinse. If the area is very greasy, spread paste of baking soda and water. Leave on for about an hour. Rinse. If this doesn't work, use mixture of powdered cleanser with chlorine bleach. Leave 10 minutes. Rinse.

Washable wallpaper

Follow package instructions on special liquid wallpaper cleaner. Check that paper is washable first. Work from the bottom up using a light touch so paper doesn't loosen. Follow design direction.

Non-washable wallpaper

Use wallpaper cleaner dough or art gum dry pads following directions on the package. Use a gentle touch so the paper isn't loosened. Remove greasy areas or crayon marks with a commercial spot remover or mineral spirits. **Test first!**

Vinyl or Coated Wall Coverings

Use dry detergent suds made from light-duty liquid detergent.

Fabric Wall Coverings

Dust with brush attachment of vacuum. Use special spot remover following package directions. Try on hidden spot first. To remove stains from uncoated burlap and silk, you need a professional. For burlap, you might risk sponging on a mild liquid detergent or a dry-cleaning fluid. Try on hidden spot first. Felt can be cleaned with granular rug cleaner. Test cleaner first. Don't use water!

Wood Walls

Coat raw wood or other unfinished paneling so moisture won't penetrate and is easier to clean. Dust frequently with soft cloth or vacuum attachment. Follow the grain of the wood. Use a solvent, liquid cleaning wax, or Murphy's Oil Soap. Follow package directions. Apply sparingly with sponge. Dry-buff with cleaning cloth, going with the grain of the wood. Don't use a solvent or solvent based cleaner or water abrasives.

Cork Walls

Fine abrasive sandpaper can clean away small marks on the surface. Rewax with solvent-based product yearly. **DO NOT** damp-mop! Seal cork with polyurethane for easier cleaning.

WOODWORK/DOORS

Don't forget that doors are a part of the woodwork too. Fingerprints and black marks need to be removed regularly. Door handles need cleaning too!

Painted

Dust often using a dry cloth or a lightly dampened cloth. Use wood cleaner following package directions if washing is needed. Don't spill, or wipe adjacent surfaces.

Wood

Dust often. If more cleaning is needed, use a wood cleaner, being careful not to spill on other surfaces; wipe immediately if spills occur. Touch up fingerprints or marks with wood cleaner such as Murphy's Oil Soap. (Follow package instructions.) Buff to dry.

WINDOWS

Clean in the morning, but not in bright sunlight since windows dry too fast and streak. Many cleaning solutions are available, but the solution and process used by professionals is:

- Mix 1/2 c ammonia, 1/2 c white vinegar, and 1 gal of warm water.
- Wet window with the solution using a sponge or a wand applicator.
- Damp wipe the blade of a squeegee (use 10- to 14-inch blade) and slide horizontally across top of window at an angle. Wipe blade each time you draw it across the window using a damp cloth.
- Place the squeegee in the dry area just created and pull vertically or horizontally. Overlap.
- Do not remove the drops that are left at the edge of the window. Let them dry.
- Wipe the windowsill with your damp cloth.

Special Problems

- Rub acid rain marks and scratches with non-gel toothpaste or automobile rubbing compound on damp sponge. Rub in direction of the scratches. Wipe with dry towel. Finish with window cleaner.
- Remove adhesive from masking tape with paint thinner, lighter fluid, or commercial tape remover.
- Remove Christmas snow film with vinegar, or 1 part ammonia mixed with 3 parts water.
- Remove paint with fingernail polish remover or turpentine. Leave on until softened. Scrape dampened window with credit card or special paint scraper using new razor blade.

- Remove hard water spots with oven-cleaning spray spritzed lightly on a dry cloth. (Be careful of your hands. Read the label!) Allow it to set briefly. Wipe off. Special cleaners are available.
- Clean Plexiglass with a solution of dishwasher detergent and water, Plexiglass fish tank cleaner, or Plexiglas windshield cleaner. Never use a dry cloth. Fill tiny nicks with clear fingernail polish.

Windowsills

If the windowsill needs extra cleaning, vacuum first. Wipe aluminum sills with liquid abrasive cleaner. For water spots, use fine steel wool or diluted rubbing alcohol. (Don't use ammonia on aluminum.) A spray-on furniture polish or wood cleaner can be used on wooden sill. Don't use water-based cleaner. Aluminum and wood sills can be waxed with car paste wax for easier cleaning.

Sliding doors

Adjust sliding doors if needed by adjusting screws on side of frame. Wash dirt off track, lubricate track with dry-silicone or Teflon-based lubricant.

Screens

Screens can be removed and cleaned outside. Lay them flat (best on soft cloth or old rug). Scrub gently with soft-bristle brush. Rinse with hose. Rap lightly to release excess water. Dry in sun.
- Screens can also be washed in the bathtub.
- Wire screens can be cleaned in place using a foaming bathroom cleaner. Spray. Leave on for a few minutes. Rinse. Do not use on nylon screens.

WINDOW COVERINGS

Curtains

Curtains can usually be machine washed according to labels on curtains. For cotton and cotton blends, you can spray starch when ironing. If there is no label on curtains, presoak very dirty curtains for 5-10 minutes before washing. Wash on gentle cycle in clean warm water with appropriate detergent. Dry on regular cycle for cotton or Permanent Press cycle for synthetics. Remove promptly. Press if needed.
- If fabric is dingy, try a nylon whitener. Nothing but redying can help sun-faded curtains.

- If curtains are just dusty, shaking them may be enough. The wand of a vacuum can be helpful.
- Don't wash curtains of synthetics like polyester or nylon in hot water. Rehang while they are damp.
- Fiberglass should soak in detergent in lukewarm water in bath or laundry tub. Swish gently. Rinse well. Hang to drip dry. (**Rinse tub to get rid of glass fibers.**)

Draperies

Vacuum drapes with upholstery attachment or remove hooks and air dry in dryer for 10-15 minutes. Rehang immediately. They often need only to have dust removed. If drapes need cleaning, follow directions on label. If draperies are washable, follow directions on the label. If the lining is a different fabric from that used in the drape, follow the directions for the most delicate of the fabrics. If draperies need dry-cleaning, take them to your local dry-cleaner. Drapes that have gone several years without cleaning may tear because they have deteriorated in sun and heat.
- For rubberized backing or vinyl laminated drapes, follow care label directions. If label isn't available, wash in lukewarm water with granular laundry detergent. If heavily soiled, presoak, changing water before washing. Dry in dryer on Permanent Press cycle and remove immediately when done.

Venetian, Levolar, or Mini-blinds

Dry-dust by closing blind and wiping with lightly water-misted, clean dust cloth. Turn louvers in opposite direction and dust again. When louvers are closed, all can be dusted at the same time.

To wash blinds, do them all at once. Open blinds so light shows. Pull to the top. Remove from brackets. Wrap cords so they won't tangle. Take outdoors. Open so louvers lay flat. Place on heavy canvas or old rug on flat surface such as a cement driveway. Scrub with soft-bristled brush dipped in an ammonia solution. Get in between the ribbons or cords. Turn blind over so other side is up. Repeat process. Hang blind on ladder or clothesline or have someone hold it. Rinse with hose. Shake. Dry. Blinds can also be dipped into ammonia solution in a bathtub. Take blinds down as directed above. Open blind. Scrub with soft bristle brush if needed. Rinse. Hang to dry.

Plastic Roll-Up Shades

Remove shade from bracket and unroll on a clean, flat, waterproof surface. Wipe with detergent solution and rinse well. Dry with clean cloth. Turn and repeat process on other side. Allow shade to stay open so it dries completely before rerolling.

ACCESSORIES

General Accessories
(frames, bookends, porcelains, ceramics, etc.)

Most accessories just need to be dusted with treated soft cloth.

- **Crystal, pottery, or porcelain** should be washed in sudsy solution when needed.
- **Metal items** should be cleaned with appropriate cleaner, reading instructions. (Brass may have a protective finish which can be destroyed with cleaners.)
- **Outside of telephone** should be cleaned with cloth dampened with detergent or cleaner solution.

Lampshades

Dust with vacuum cleaner attachments or dry cloth. If washable, launder in lukewarm suds. (Bathtub is good place.) Rinse. Avoid hard scrubbing. Pat dry with absorbent towel. Hang to dry. (Use fan to hurry drying and avoiding rust.) If not washable, follow manufacturer's instructions. Usually can clean with non-flammable dry-cleaning fluid or art gum eraser. Be gentle.

INSECT CONTROL

Outside House

- Keep areas around house free of decaying debris where rodents and insects live.
- Caulk all areas on outside of house where bugs can enter.
- Keep tight lids on garbage containers. Use plastic liners. Keep containers clean.
- Keep windows and screens in good repair.

Inside House

- Keep floor registers, heating and cooling ducts clean.
- Treat clothes of animal fibers such as wool with moth-proofing insecticide or brush and store in cedar. (Clean under collars and lapels, in pockets, inside cuffs and seams.)
- Don't keep stacks of papers and magazines, especially in damp areas.
- Use vacuum or brush to remove dust and lint from cracks, crevices, corners, and baseboards.
- Repair leaks and use dehumidifier in damp areas that attract insects.
- Get rid of waste food promptly to avoid odors that attract vermin and insects.
- Keep interiors of garbage cans clean.
- Keep cereals and other grain products in tightly covered containers.
- Move heavy furniture and appliances away from walls and keep them clean underneath.

Insecticides

- Use insecticides following directions on containers only if needed. Call exterminator for severe problems. (Airborne insecticides destroy flying insects on contact and kill crawling insects hit directly. Surface insecticides are applied to surfaces where insects crawl.)
- Treat entry and pathway used by crawling pests.
- If cupboard area is infested, remove contents and dispose of contaminated foods. Clean interior with disinfectant solution. Apply surface insecticide to seams and corners using package directions. Dry. Line surfaces with paper. Be careful around foods so that they aren't contaminated.

Traveling to See New Horizons

"How can I plan to see more of the world?"

There's a whole world out there just waiting to be explored. If the "sand in your shoes" needs to be emptied, a good time to do it is before you "settle down." Travel and vacations may be a part of your goals. Fitting them into a limited budget can be challenging, but possible. Traveling can be expensive or inexpensive depending on your choices.

Planning A Vacation

#1 Consider different kinds of alternatives

You might like to consider something new like vacations on riverboats, houseboats, ranches, and farms. The outdoors takes you backpacking, horseback riding, bicycling, and camping. Universities offer unusual vacation plans. Hostels in this country and in foreign countries offer inexpensive housing. There are tours by bus or train. Some museums even offer archeological digs. There are also houses to be swapped.

#2 Gather Information

- Research library resources: travel books, travel guides, travel sections of newspapers.
- Write Chambers of Commerce or national embassies for information on activities and accommodations.
- Talk with tourist bureaus and travel agents.
- Use Compuserve and Internet.

#3 Plan your route, activities, and accommodations

If you drive or bicycle, get good maps and plan your route before you begin your plans. Maps are important to help you get to and around in cities. If you want help, use:

- Motor clubs such as AAA to plan routes and give travel information (only for members.)
- Travel guides available at stores and libraries for planning, sightseeing, and accommodations.
- Travel agents if using public transportation. Explain what you want and time and money limits. They schedule travel arrangements, reserve accommodations and car rentals, find less costly ways, and schedule travel details (i.e. insurance, passports and visas, immunizations required, customs, import duties, and weather).

#4 Make your own reservations for accommodations

You can use 800 numbers of large motel chains in the Yellow Pages of your telephone directory. There should also be a directory of 800 numbers in your library. Guide books can suggest motels and B&Bs (Bed and Breakfast) with their price listings. Plan and call ahead to avoid disappointments. Computer programs can be used for making reservations too. Check camping guides to see if camping sites need reservations. You may need to write or call ahead.

Foreign and US Travel

Traveling can be very broadening and exciting. Research all that you can before you plan your trip. You can talk to persons who have lived or visited where you want to go. Information at the library will be helpful. Much of the fun of any trip can be learning about the area and people before you go. Background is not only interesting but it is helpful, especially in a different culture if you choose to go abroad.

Luggage/Packing

- Take only what you need, since you must carry all of it.
- Plan to wash some things and allow them to dry overnight. Be sure the pieces you carry dry quickly.
- Take clothes that mix and match, are lightweight, and won't wrinkle. Include enough variety to take you wherever you want to go. Just jeans probably won't be enough!
- Leave space in luggage for purchases. You can also carry a small, collapsible bag to use on return.
- Leave valuables such as jewelry at home, especially if they are not replaceable.
- Tag each luggage piece with your name and address. Put your name and address, and a business address inside each piece.
- Keep the luggage locked.

Traveler's Checks

Traveler's checks are a safe way to carry money. Copy each serial number two times. Take one set with you. (Carry the numbers in a different place than you carry the checks.) Leave the other set at home. Keep track of the traveler's checks that you cash. Countersign only in front of person cashing the check.

Use of Traveler's Checks in Foreign Countries

- Plan your check cashing time carefully. Banks, border currency exchanges, airport, or train stations may be closed when you need them. Plan for holidays, since business places will be closed.
- Cash traveler's checks only in the amount that you plan to spend. There is a charge for conversion of money when entering or leaving a country.
- Use commercial banks or major currency exchanges for best rates of exchange. Restaurants and hotels, though convenient, have much higher rates.
- If you purchase traveler's checks in your host country, cash them before leaving.
- Countersign traveler's checks only in front of the person cashing them.

Money/Personal Checks in U.S.

- Don't flash the money you have at any time! This invites thieves.
- Personal checks are hard to cash. An ATM card is useful. Money works best, but can be lost.

Use of Money/Personal Checks in Foreign Countries

- American dollars are fine currency and acceptable in some places, but generally the local host country money is necessary for purchases. Money exchanges are at most airports, train or bus stations.
- Don't plan to use personal checks. They are usually not acceptable even at banks.
- Exchange rates are posted in bank windows. Rates are identified with flags of the countries.
- Carry a hand-held calculator to help with money exchange and purchases.
- If you can, make arrangements through U.S. banks to take some foreign cash with you. (It's costly.)
- Carry all valuables carefully hidden, preferably inside clothing. Don't flash money.

Credit Cards

- Take only credit cards you will use. If you have more than one card, carry in separate place.
- Check your credit limit and don't exceed it!
- Check the expiration date on credit card before you leave. Check early enough to get a new one.
- Photocopy credit cards that you take. Copy the numbers and names of the cards, and the phone number of the place where you should report a lost credit card. Leave one set of these copies at home with someone whom you can contact in case of loss. Carry second set of copies with you. Separate them from other valuables so they don't get stolen at the same time.
- Be sure to get your credit card returned after using it!
- Some credit cards allow you to save money on car rentals by use of their insurance, even in other countries.

Use of Credit Cards in Foreign Country

- Credit cards are usually used to your benefit if the rates are stable or climbing. If the U.S. dollar is declining in value, you may end up paying more for it than if you paid cash.
- ATM cards are becoming an acceptable way to get money when traveling internationally.

Passports/Visas for Foreign Countries

- When you leave the United States, passports are normally necessary to allow you to enter or leave a country. Get directions from your local post office or a passport agency. Passports take time to process, so plan to get them at least two months before you need them. A passport requires a fee. You must apply in person and bring: copy of birth certificate or naturalization papers, another identification with your signature (i.e. driver's license), two recent, duplicate 2x2-inch passport photographs.
- Sometimes visas are necessary for countries you visit. These requirements change regularly, so check.
- Make two copies of your passport identification page and visa. Leave one at home and carry the other in a separate place from your real passport in case of loss. Make a copy of your airline tickets too.

Driving in a Foreign Country

An international driver's license is helpful if you plan to rent a car. These licenses may be required in some countries. Check at your local driver's license bureau or AAA office for information. A license requires a valid U.S. state driver's license, two passport-type photos, and a fee. Insurance is necessary if you rent a car. Check to see if your credit card pays for the necessary insurance. Sometimes "gold credit cards" allow this. Also check to see if your own automobile insurance covers you in a foreign country.

Safety Tips in United States and Abroad

To avoid loss of valuables:

- Make plans to keep your money, passport, visa, credit cards, and travelers' checks on your body at all times. Pickpockets are clever and skilled! Backpacks, purses hanging by straps, pockets, fanny packs, and billfolds are not safe. You can carry valuables in:
  1. Money waist bags inside your clothing.
  2. Bags around your neck on a string (best hidden inside your clothes).
  3. Small plastic or cotton bag for placing inside bra.
  4. Inside jacket pockets (only if not visible).
  5. Other less safe ways include (a) a billfold with a rubber band around it carried in a buttoned, covered pocket (b) a tightly zippered over-the-shoulder purse carried while you walk on sidewalk close to buildings with purse on side away from the street.
- Don't be distracted by small children's attentions or persons gathered around you. This can be the guise of a pickpocket group, especially in foreign countries.
- Check your insurance before your trip to see that you are covered for accidents, loss, and illness.
- Never leave valuable things in your room. Keep hotel and car keys on your person!

Protect your Luggage

- Never leave your luggage unattended. (This is especially important after you've packed for the airport. Illegal items can be placed in your

luggage and you will be held responsible. You also invite theft and bombs.)

- Be sure to get a claim check for each piece of your luggage if you check in at any public transportation.

Protect Yourself in Hotels

- Don't give your hotel room number to anyone you don't know. You can always meet in a crowded lobby, but be careful of strangers.
- Always keep your hotel door locked.
- Keep your valuables close to you at night.
- Book rooms between the second and seventh floors for fire safety.
- Leave a rented car in a safe parking lot such as those available at hotels.

Personal Safety in Foreign Countries

- Don't plan to sell your own clothing, jewelry or personal items. This may be illegal.
- Read about local customs and laws of the areas you plan to visit. This information is available in libraries, travel agencies, and tourist bureaus.
- Learn some simple phrases in the language of the host country. Carry a translating dictionary along for further help. (There is usually, fortunately, someone in most countries who speaks English.)
- Keep track of recent developments in the countries you hope to visit. Information will be available through the regional U.S. Passport Agencies and through computer services.
- Be sure to leave information at home with some contact person in case you have a problem. Include such things as medical or dental records, insurance records, up-to-date will, and a power of attorney.
- If you must carry drugs for your own medication, carry proof of their use with doctor's prescription. Do not carry any illegal drugs!
- If you need further information, you can order: *"A Safe Trip Abroad"* Department of State Publication 9493, Bureau of Consular Affairs, U.S. Government Printing Office, Washington DC 20402.

Personal Safety Hints

- Do not go into dangerous areas. Avoid dark alleys and shortcuts.
- It's best not to travel alone at night.
- Don't draw attention to yourself by flashy clothes, jewelry, or anything that will identify you as a "rich" tourist. Don't draw attention by any loud actions of conversation or argument.

What To Do If Something is Stolen

- If anything gets stolen, report the loss immediately to appropriate authorities such as police. Keep a copy of the police report for insurance purposes.
- If airline tickets are stolen, report immediately to the airlines or travel agent.
- If traveler's checks are stolen, report immediately to the issuing company or agent.

Passport Stolen in Foreign Country

- If your passport is stolen, report it immediately to the closest U.S. Embassy or Consulate.

Health Concerns

- If you need medications, carry prescriptions for refills or in case of questioning by authorities.
- Prescriptions should include generic name of drug. Carry medicines in original labeled container.
- If the medicine is a narcotic, carry a note from your physician to tell the reason for the medication.
- If you have allergies or special health problems, wear an alert on a bracelet or necklace.
- Carry a prescription for your glasses or contacts as well as a duplicate pair for emergencies.

Health Concerns in Foreign Countries

Check with passport agencies, travel agencies, embassies, or computer resource for update on immunizations required for countries you intend to visit. Also check for advisories of any adverse conditions abroad, including violence.

Buying Wheels

"How can I choose a good car?"

If you want to save money and headaches, avoid impulse buying and make a plan. Arm yourself with information.

#1 Look at your budget

Consider what you can afford for actual purchase and down payment. Include the trade-in value of your present car if you have one. You can find the value of new or used cars by checking with a bank or credit union or researching library books such as the *Kelly Blue Book Used Car Guide* or *Edmunds New Car Prices*. Read magazines such as *Consumer Reports, Popular Mechanix* and *Motor Trend*. The wholesale price is the price dealers normally pay for trade-ins in good condition. The retail price is the price the dealer will try to get for your car when sold. If you sell the car yourself, you may get more money than a dealer will offer.

Consider all costs of owning a car including an emergency fund for unexpected repairs. You can check normal costs in the library by reading *Cost of Owning and Operating Automobiles* by the U.S. Department of Transportation or *The Complete Car Cost Guide* by IntelliChoice, Inc.

Age of car: Generally you will be much further ahead financially with a used car, wisely chosen. New cars depreciate rapidly the first year.

Fuel cost: Consider the miles you'll drive, miles per gallon the car uses, and gasoline type and cost. (Formula: Miles driven per year divided by average miles per gallon multiplied by price per gallon = gasoline cost per year.)

Fees and license: Since these vary, call agency that issues license plates.

Taxes: These vary from state to state. They can include such things as sales tax, excise tax, and personal property tax. Check with tax people or car dealers.

Insurance: Call several insurance agents to compare costs. Learn about suggested coverage as you talk (see page 14). Insurance costs vary with the make of the car.

Finance costs: Call financial institutions before you shop to check costs. See if there are any added service charges and extra insurance to cover loan.

Financial Institution	Advantages	Disadvantages
Auto dealers	Convenient	Generally higher costs than other institutions. Loans often sold to other companies. Less control if things go wrong.
Banks/ Savings & Loans	Reasonable rates	Down payment or collateral is usually required.
Credit Unions	Low rates	Must be credit union member. Down payment may be required.
Finance Companies	Easy credit	Very high rates to cover risks. Extra service charges are usually required.
Personal/family	No credit rating	Family takes risk. May cause problems with family relationships.

Estimate the total cost of ownership to see what you can afford.

Purchase price	$_____
Finance costs	_____
Insurance	_____
Registration fees	_____
License plates	_____
Maintenance (tires, oil, etc.)	_____
Initial repairs	_____
Gasoline per year	_____
Miscellaneous (parking, etc.)	_____
Emergency fund	_____
TOTAL	$_____

#2 List what you want in a car. Choose two or three models that meet your needs.

Research to find the real costs of these potential models and check their repair records. Talk to people, read ads, visit car agencies, ask bankers, credit unions, and car dealers. Read in books and magazines suggested above. Create a list of "extras" that you want if you buy a new car so you won't be tempted to accept others not needed.

#3 Comparison shop for a car *without buying.*

- Consider the location of the dealer and the quality of service offered.
- Test drive your choices for at least 15 minutes using congested areas and highway.
- Take notes as you look.
- **Don't sign anything until you're ready to buy.** Avoid impulse buying! Salespeople will prefer that you sign a tentative sales agreement before they get to real pricing. **Don't sign anything until you're ready to buy and have comparative shopped!**
- Reread this full chapter to avoid sales tricks and scams.
- If looking for a new car:

  -Check the *Consumers Report* for actual costs including "extras." This will show you the pricing structure including extra accessories so you can bargain wisely. Get a detailed list of the dealer cost for car and options from Consumer Reports New Car Price Service (1-800-933-5555) for a small charge.

  -Compare prices of competitors in different areas.

  -Compare cost of leasing versus financing.
- If looking for a used car:

  -Ask for name of previous owners and call them. Find what work has been done and what problems there are. (A dealer should give you the name if you ask.)

  -Recheck the used car guides to find the real value of your car if you trade it in.

  -Carefully check the car using the listing below.

  -Test drive the car.

  -When you find the used car you can afford, take it to a trusted mechanic, a diagnostic center or a dealership that sells the same make of car to get an estimate for repairs needed. Tell them any findings observed while looking at or driving the car. Don't rely on the word of the maintenance department where you are buying the car.

WHAT TO LOOK FOR IN A USED CAR

A CHECK LIST FOR PURCHASING A USED CAR

Body:
- No ripples, paint shade differences, dents, welding spots, breaks in frame, paint flaking
- Doors don't sag when opened
- No rust spots including door bottoms and rear fenders
- Doors, trunk and hood work easily and fit properly
- No breaks or chips in windshield, glass, or lights
- Car is level when viewed from 10 feet behind
- Car bounces several times when corner of car is pushed up and down (good shock absorbers)
- Tires don't shake much when shaken at the top
- When viewed from the rear while car is driven, front and back wheels line up and car body is at the same angle as where it is being driven

Mechanics:
- Oil dipstick is clear when rubbed with fingers showing no visible dirt or grit (analysis is available)
- Lubrication record stickers indicate proper changes (oil changed by owner has no stickers.)
- Transmission fluid clear with no burnt odor
- Battery not corroded or cracked
- Clutch doesn't grab, chatter or indicate too much play when shifting
- No noise when automatic transmission is accelerating
- Car doesn't overheat when driving
- When driving on bumpy road, no rattles, squeaks, poor steering
- When driving on straight road, no pull to right or left
- No black, sooty oil deposits on exhaust tail pipe
- No white or blue smoke from exhaust when car is in neutral and gas pedal is pushed down
- Brake doesn't sink slowly when pressed
- When turning steering wheel from side to side it doesn't turn more than a few inches before wheels turn
- Steering wheel doesn't bind or feel loose when turning
- Air conditioning blows cold air. Heater blows warm air
- Window washer, turn signals, radio, horn, fuel gauge, warning light, and horn work

Tires:
- Wear is appropriate to the mileage driven
- Show even wear with no scuff marks on inside
- All match each other
- No evidence of brake fluid on inside wheels and walls
- Good spare tire
- There is wheel changing equipment

Interior:
- Upholstery and floors in good shape
- Pedals not badly worn
- Seat belts work
- Odometer shows no white lines between numerals that indicate it's been turned back

Under:
- No rotten egg smell to indicate catalytic converter problem
- Muffler exhaust pipe, and tail pipe connected and no rust
- No oil or transmission fluid spots

WHERE TO LOOK FOR USED CARS

Used car lots (Find one that's been in business for a long time.)
New car dealers (They usually keep only the best used cars to sell.)
Newspaper ads
Friends (But watch the price!)
Banks and finance companies (For repossessions.)
Rental car agencies

HOW TO PROTECT YOURSELF WHEN BUYING

Understand Sales Tricks

Beware of sales techniques. Salespeople are trained in psychological selling. They tell you what you want to hear. They listen, ask questions, and answer questions with questions. They sell to your emotions and senses. **Talk little to reduce sales maneuvers.** Salespersons get hints of how to sell to you as you speak.

The "extras," especially on new cars, offer confusing costs. One protection is to place a special order that includes only what you want.

Deals on Wheels, How to Buy, Care For and Sell a Car by former auto dealer Gordon Page is a good book to research sales techniques of car salesmen.

Watch Out for Scams

•**Bait and switch** is a method of advertising at a very low price. When persons come to buy, they are told the car has been sold or is not available. Then salesperson tries to sell something else.

•**Loss leaders** are cars that have been stripped and advertised at a low price. Salesperson tries to sell a different car.

•**Low ball** is a method of advertising a very low price, possibly below cost to the dealer. This method encourages the buyer to return ready to buy, but the real price which is much higher will then be quoted.

•**High ball** offers a customer a very high trade-in for a car. This encourages the customer to return and the difference is made up in different ways.

WHEN TO BUY

- When salesrooms are least busy such as early on a week-day, holidays (especially Christmas), and in good weather in spring or fall. Go when other people don't want to go such as in bad weather.

- When models are changing.
- When economic times or local economy is weak.
- When special promotions are happening and there are sales contests for salespersons.
- When competition is keen between sellers.
- When salespeople are trying to meet their monthly goals at the end of the month.

#4 Comparison shop and *Really Buy*

- It's best to ask the salesperson if he/she is qualified to make the sale. If not, get the sales manager to participate from the start of your negotiating. Follow salesperson who goes to check price with manager. (He/she may be going for a cup of coffee!)
- Read and understand every word in any presale or final sale contract before signing.
- When buying a used car, ask for lower price if car is sold "as is." (Consider carefully!)
- If buying a new car, let salesperson know that you are aware of what dealer paid for the car.
- Make a list of answers such as prices as you talk. (This makes the salesperson more cautious.) It is valuable to look prepared with all information in a notebook that you use.
- Ask for lowest possible price and make sure price won't change later. Stick to the price you are willing to pay.
- Don't mention trade-in until after first price is reached without one. Then ask for a new price with your trade-in. (The difference of these two prices is the actual allowance for your car.) This is the time to decide if you want to sell it yourself.
- Bargain with salesperson to get lowest possible price.
- On a new car purchase, be careful of the manipulation of "optional extras" pricing. Consider placing a special order for a car that has only the accessories that you feel you want.
- **Don't be bullied or rushed. Don't be afraid to walk out!**

Other Things To Check Before Signing Contract for Purchase

- Get everything in writing. Make sure there are no blank spaces in forms. Check for accuracy.
- Make sure title is clear. Get the title when you get the car. (Consider the possibility that the car may be stolen. You are at risk if owner finds it. Generally dealers have insurance for this possibility. Private sellers don't.)
- Understand warranty coverage including length of time or miles covered. Check if warranty can be transferred. Also see if warranties of previous owners are transferrable to you (i.e. tires, repairs).
- Have repairs made before purchase and payment.
- Understand all costs of all add-ons.
- Check for lowest cost loans by comparing. (When setting up loan, pay the largest payments you can afford to cut cost of interest. Also see if you can pay the loan early.)

> Be sure you have the car insured before driving it off the lot.

Selling Your Own Car Yourself

If you sell your car by yourself consider the following:

- Check with state motor vehicle department about licensing, title transfer, and taxes.
- Write up a bill of sale with your name, car's serial number, and cost.
- Notify your insurance company to cancel your policy after sale is complete and title is transferred .
- **Stay safe!** Don't allow people into your house if they make you uncomfortable. Always have someone with you. If you receive a telephone call from someone answering your ad, get name, address, and telephone number of the person. Repeat number for accuracy. Call the person back to plan an appointment. (This allows you to trace the person if necessary.)

- Don't give car or title to purchaser until all legal arrangements are completed. When arranging payment make sure the check, even a certified one, is good. Note on the receipt of purchase that the sale is contingent on a good check. It's best to get the money in your hands first! If you consider letting the buyer take over your payments, check directly with both buyer and your lender to see that you aren't liable for payments any longer.
- Before letting someone drive the car, check person's driver's license and make notes including the license number. Be sure to go along with the person testing the car. You are responsible if there is an accident.

Protecting from Overcharging on Repairs

- Since state laws differ on repair process payment, check local laws through an appropriate agency such as the Department of Transportation.
- Comparison shop when choosing a reputable repair mechanic. (Ask people for recommendations. Check Better Business Bureau.) When you've chosen one, take a list of problems to share with the mechanic or person who writes up the order.
- Get a cost estimate for tentative repairs.
- Request that you be notified if charges will be higher than estimate given.
- Check to see the repair order describes the work requested accurately and get a copy of it. (Communicate directly with mechanic and have a repair order early if you plan to leave the car before or after business hours.)
- Request an itemized bill for each part replaced and have the mechanic save the parts.
- Keep itemized receipts for future reference. (Especially important if car is under warranty.)
- If there's a warranty on repairs, get a signed and dated guarantee.

Saving Transportation Dollars

Taking Care of Automobile

- Keep tires inflated to pressure suggested in manual, checking when tires are cool.
- Keep wheels aligned.
- Follow all manual instructions and stay close to suggested schedules for maintenance including air and oil filter changes.
- Check tension on fan belt.
- Keep battery filled with water. Wash terminals with baking soda and water using rubber gloves and brush.
- Fill with antifreeze for summer and winter.
- Keep exterior clean and protected, washing salt off under body regularly.
- Keep interior clean. Wash vinyl and vacuum rugs.

Driving Tips To Save Gasoline

- Accelerate and brake smoothly. Don't "jack rabbit" start or dart in and out of traffic.
- Accelerate a bit before starting up a hill. Release gas pedal at top of hill to allow gravity to help.
- Drive at a steady speed.
- Avoid extra weight in car.
- Coast to stop if light is turning red. Don't use brakes unless necessary.
- Keep windows closed if possible.
- Drive only when necessary. Plan ahead to carpool, consolidate trips, walk, or bicycle.
- Use air-conditioning only when necessary.

Yearly Financial Plan

FIXED EXPENSES:	Month 1 Planned	Actual	Month 2 Planned	Actual	Month 3 Planned	Actual	Month 4 Planned	Actual
Social Security								
Rent								
Taxes								
Loans								
Credit card payments								
Savings								
Emergency fund*								
Reserve fund*								
Utilities: Gas/Electricity								
Telephone								
Pledges								
Renter's insurance								
Auto insurance								
Life insurance								
Medical insurance								
Water								
Other								
FLEXIBLE EXPENSES								
Food								
Eating out								
Clothing								
Transportation, bus								
Automobile expenses								
Recreation								
Laundry/cleaning								
Newspapers/books								
Tuitions/education								
Books/supplies								
Dues								
Furnishings								
Cleaning supplies								
Personal care								
Hobbies								
Gifts								
Vacations								
Medical expenses								
Other								
Total for months								

* Especially as you are beginning, it is important to start building an emergency fund for unexpected expenses and a reserve fund for periodic expenses that are paid in lumps rather than monthly.

Yearly Financial Plan

FIXED EXPENSES:	Month 1 Planned	Actual	Month 2 Planned	Actual	Month 3 Planned	Actual	Month 4 Planned	Actual
Social Security								
Rent								
Taxes								
Loans								
Credit card payments								
Savings								
Emergency fund*								
Reserve fund*								
Utilities: Gas/Electricity								
Telephone								
Pledges								
Renter's insurance								
Auto insurance								
Life insurance								
Medical insurance								
Water								
Other								
FLEXIBLE EXPENSES								
Food								
Eating out								
Clothing								
Transportation, bus								
Automobile expenses								
Recreation								
Laundry/cleaning								
Newspapers/books								
Tuitions/education								
Books/supplies								
Dues								
Furnishings								
Cleaning supplies								
Personal care								
Hobbies								
Gifts								
Vacations								
Medical expenses								
Other								
Total for months								

* Especially as you are beginning, it is important to start building an emergency fund for unexpected expenses and a reserve fund for periodic expenses that are paid in lumps rather than monthly.

Yearly Financial Plan

FIXED EXPENSES:	Month 1 Planned	Actual	Month 2 Planned	Actual	Month 3 Planned	Actual	Month 4 Planned	Actual
Social Security								
Rent								
Taxes								
Loans								
Credit card payments								
Savings								
Emergency fund*								
Reserve fund*								
Utilities: Gas/Electricity								
Telephone								
Pledges								
Renter's insurance								
Auto insurance								
Life insurance								
Medical insurance								
Water								
Other								
FLEXIBLE EXPENSES								
Food								
Eating out								
Clothing								
Transportation, bus								
Automobile expenses								
Recreation								
Laundry/cleaning								
Newspapers/books								
Tuitions/education								
Books/supplies								
Dues								
Furnishings								
Cleaning supplies								
Personal care								
Hobbies								
Gifts								
Vacations								
Medical expenses								
Other								
Total for months								

* Especially as you are beginning, it is important to start building an emergency fund for unexpected expenses and a reserve fund for periodic expenses that are paid in lumps rather than monthly.

Yearly Financial Plan Summary

EXPENSE	Planned	Actual
Social Security		
Rent		
Taxes		
Loans		
Credit card payments		
Savings		
Emergency fund*		
Reserve fund*		
Utilities: Gas/Electricity		
Telephone		
Pledges		
Renter's insurance		
Auto insurance		
Life insurance		
Medical insurance		
Water		
Other		
FLEXIBLE EXPENSES		
Food		
Eating out		
Lunches at work		
Clothing		
Transportation, bus		
Automobile expenses		
Recreation		
Laundry/cleaning		
Newspapers/books		
Tuitions/education		
Books/supplies		
Dues		
Furnishings		
Cleaning supplies		
Personal care		
Hobbies		
Gifts		
Vacations		
Medical expenses		
Other		
Total for months		

SUMMARY

Total income

Monthly average fixed expenses

Subtract to get amount available for flexible expenses

Yearly Financial Plan Summary

Total Income $_____

Minus the

     Total Fixed & Flexible Expenses   −_____

Balance $_____ *

* If this balance is negative, you have work to do to reset your priorities or goals. If it is positive, you can add to your savings, emergency fund or investments.

INFORMAL ROOMMATE CONTRACT

FINANCES

Address of unit to be rented _____

Date agreement begins _____

                          (Month)   (Date)   (Year)

I.   Roommates renting unit:

    Roommate #1 _____

      Present Address _____

    Roommate #2 _____

      Present Address _____

    Roommate #3 _____

      Present Address _____

II. Rent: (Check appropriate statement and complete or mark out blank lines)

    Rent amount for the unit is _____ per_____

    Date when rent payment is due _____

    This rent payment includes the following utilities: _____

    _____

    _____

III. Utilities: (Check appropriate statement and complete or mark out blank lines)

    Utilities not covered by rent:

    ❑ Gas bill will be paid by (name) _____

      Names on billing will include: _____

    ❑ Electricity bill will be paid by (name) _____

      Names on billing will include: _____

    ❑ Water/sewer bill will be paid by (name) _____

      Names on billing will include: _____

    ❑ Other utility bills (explain): _____

      Will be paid by (name) _____

      Names on billing will include: _____

    ❑ **All persons will share equally in the payment of rent and utilities.**

IV. Telephone: (Check appropriate statement and complete or mark out blank lines)

    ❑ Telephone bill will be paid by (name)_____

      Names on billing will include: _____

    _____

    ❑ Each roommate will pay equal portion of base bill.

    ❑ Each roommate will pay his/her personal long distance calls.

V. Security deposit:

_____ will pay_____

_____ will pay_____

_____ will pay_____

The amounts will be paid back when security deposit is returned when he/she moves out.

VI. **Moving out:**

When a roommate moves, _____days notice will be given. If proper notice isn't given, the roommate must pay his/her share of rent until the notice period is up.

When moving out: (Check appropriate spaces)

_____ All roommates agree to move out at same time on: Date_____

_____ If, for any reason, a roommate must move, he/she will continue to pay his/her share of rent and bills to end of lease.

_____ If, for any reason, a roommate moves before lease ends, he/she may replace self with a substitute roommate that is agreed upon by remaining roommates. No financial loss should be left for the remaining roommates.

_____ If any damage is done to the unit, whoever caused the damage must pay for it.

_____ Cleaning up process will be shared before anyone moves.

_____ If there are costs that will be charged from the security deposit, each roommate will pay his/her share.

_____ Other:_____

_____

VII. **Food:**

_____ Each roommate will buy his/her own food.

_____ Groceries will be purchased and shared equally.

_____ Personal food will be "borrowed" only with permission and will be paid for or replaced as agreed.

_____ Other: _____

_____

VIII. **Shared equipment and furnishings:**

The shared furnishings will be handled as follows when roommates move out:

Equipment	Original cost	Who will pay share & keep	Who will sell & split proceeds

Damage done to shared furnishings should be repaired or paid for by mutual agreement.

IX. **Renter's insurance:**

(This insurance should be carefully checked with your insurance agent!)

_____Renter's insurance will be paid for by (name)_____

The insurance will be paid directly to _____

_____

Other plan: _____

_____

SPACE SHARING AGREEMENTS

Laundry:

Each roommate will do his/her personal laundry at_____

Shared laundry will be handled in the following manner:_____

_____

JOB SHARING AGREEMENTS

Job	When to be done (week, day, etc.)	Done by

Quiet hours for radio, TV, stereo, etc. are:_____Weekdays _____Weekends

Guests: Overnight guest limits_____ Number_____ How often_____

Other guest limits_____ Number_____ How often_____

Hobby Limits:

Hobbies_____

Limits _____

FURNISHINGS INVENTORY AND PREPLANNING

Decorating Style Preferred (circle)

Cottage/Farmhouse   Country   Town House   International   Minimal   Eclectic

Color preference _____

Size of room(s)   #1_____   #2_____   #3_____   #4_____

How I'll use the room(s)
(i.e. study, entertain,
sleep, hobby)

#1_____
#2_____
#3_____
#4_____

Furnishings I Have

Furnishing	Color	Size	Repair needed	Cost

Furnishings I Need

Furniture	Color	Date needed	Cost

Appliances I Have

Appliance	Color	Repair needed	Cost

Appliances I Need

Appliances	Date needed	Cost

Accessories I Have

Accessory	Color	Repair needed	Cost

Accessories I Need

Accessories	Date needed	Cost

Equipment I Have

Equipment	Color	Repair needed	Cost

Equipment I Need

Accessories	Date needed	Cost

Bibliography

American Express. **Getting Started.** NY NY: American Express World Financial Center, 1988

Browne, Mona R.D. **Label Facts for Healthful Eating.** Dayton, O: Mazer Corp., 1994

Caughey, V. Marie. **Decisions for Independent Living.** Peoria, IL: Bennett Publishing Co. 1982

College for Financial Planning. **High School Financial Planning Program.** College for Financial Planning in partnership with U.S. Dept. of Agricultural Extension Service and Cooperative Extension System. September. 1992

Cooperative Extension Service. **Caring for Your Carpet.** NCR 462. Columbus MO: Publications Office Cooperative Extension Service, 1993

Dunn, Charlotte M. **Storage and Temperature Table.** Madison, WI: University of Wisconsin Extension, 1975

Department of State. **Your Trip Abroad.** Washington DC: Department of State Publications 9926, 1992

"Smart Car Buying Strategies." **Family Circle** (October 11, 1994)

Florman, Monte, and Marjorie Florman. **How to Clean Practically Anything.** Yonkers NY: Consumer Report Books, 1993

IntelliChoice, Inc. **The Complete Car Cost Guide.** San Jose CA: IntelliChoice, Inc., 1991

Johnson Wax. **Home Care.** ED 501RI. Racine WI: Consumer Service Center
   Furniture Care. ED 301R3. Racine WI: Consumer Service Center

Lipman, Ira A. **How to Protect Yourself from Crime.** NY NY: Avon Books, The Hearst Corporation, 1982

Money Management Institute. **Your Clothing Dollar.** Prospect Heights, IL: Household International, 1983
   Your Recreation Dollar. Prospect Heights, IL: Houshold International, 1981

Morton, John S., and Ronald R. Resny. **Consumer Action.** Atlanta: Houghton Mifflin Co ., 1983

National Coalition for Consumer Educators. **What Consumers Should Know About Health Care Services and Health Insurance.** Washington DC: Community and Consumer Relations Health Insurance Association of America

Page, Gordon. **Deals on Wheels, How to Buy, Care for and Sell a Car.** Brookfield, WI: Page Publishing, 1983

Proctor and Gamble Educational Services. **Learning About Laundering.** Cincinnati: Proctor and Gamble Co., 1983-84

Quindt, Barbara Gilder. "Better Ways to Borrow and Save." **Family Circle,** 1995

Sears. **Planning for Today and Tomorrow.** Chicago: Sears Consumer Information Services, 1974

Sohl, Joyce D. **Managing Our Money Updated.** Women's Division of United Methodist Church, 1990

"To Your Good Health—Choosing a Doctor." **Current Consumer and Lifestyle.** November, 1983

United States Department of Agriculture. **Eating Better When Eating Out Using Dietary Guidelines.** H&G Bulletin   232-11. Washington DC: U.S. Government Printing Office
   "Know Your Molds." **Food News for Consumers.** Washington DC: USDA, 1985

U.S. Department of Health and Human Services. "The ABC's of Food Storage." DHHS No(FOA) 892210, **FDA Consumer.** Washington DC: U.S. Government Printing Office, 1989

United Van Lines. **Doing Your Own Packing.** Fenton, MO: United Van Lines, 1988

Index

GIVE THE GIFT THAT LASTS A LIFETIME...

I CAN DO IT!
A Micropedia of Living On Your Own
by Marian B. Latzko, M.S., Mom, Mrs.

This gift of independent living skill information is put into the mind, into the heart and into *action* that helps young people create a quality life.

A quick, easy reference includes a wealth of information on how to:

* Budget and use money to reach goals
* Travel safely
* Clean
* Choose and care for clothing
* Stay safe from intruders/accidents
* Create a roommate contract
* Find housing and move
* Eat nutritionally "at home" or "out"
* Create a support network...even find a job
* Buy an automobile, furnishings & supplies
* Use credit wisely
* Save money
* And .... much, much more!

A perfect gift for graduations, apartment warmings, moving to a dorm, birthdays, weddings, grandchildren, leaving home . . . .to name a few.

A great teaching resource for high schools, adult education, alternative schools, parent groups, Independent Living programs, colleges, counselors, mentors and parents.

You'll want one for yourself!

High quality; 4-color laminated soft cover, 9 1/2" x 11" book with 136 pages. Illustrated by Sally Kneeland.

I CAN DO IT! A Micropedia of Living On Your Own
by Marian B. Latzko
ISBN 0-9651826-0-6

Quantity _____ @ $15.95 each   =$_____

Add $3.75 shipping and handling for 1st book   =$_____

Add $1.00 shipping and handling for each additional book
shipped to same address   =$_____

WI residents add 5% sales tax (.80 each)   =$_____

THANK YOU FOR YOUR ORDER   ORDER TOTAL   =$_____

* To order! Call toll free: 1-888-357-7654   Fax: 1-920-735-9434
or send this form and checks to:
MICROLIFE   1610 N. Briarcliff Dr.   Appleton WI   54915-2837
* Make checks payable to Microlife   *VISA & MASTERCARD accepted
* Purchase orders acceptable   (MICROLIFE will invoice organization.)

Please charge MASTERCARD or VISA (circle one) Card # _ _ _ _ _ _ _ _ _ _ _ _ _ _ _ _

Expiration Date ____/____/____   Signature_____

SHIP TO:

Name or Organization (please print)_____ PO#_____

Address_____City_____State____Zip_____

#3 Book